THINKING HORIZONTALLY

THINKING HORIZONTALLY

HOW TO EXPAND YOUR BUSINESS
THROUGH HORIZONTAL GROWTH

JAMES MANSKE

NEW DEGREE PRESS

THINKING HORIZONTALLY

How to Expand Your Business through Horizontal Growth

ISBN   978-1-63676-921-9 *Paperback*

          978-1-63676-985-1 *Kindle Ebook*

          978-1-63730-089-3 *Ebook*

Dedication

To My Loving Family....

This book is for you.

To all my mentors over the years and those who have shaped me into who I am today and who I will become in the future, I am forever grateful.

And to all my friends, colleagues, employees, and those that have contributed to the pursuit of writing this book.

Cheers

CONTENTS

___

INTRODUCTION

———

According to the Bureau of Labor Statistics' Business Employment Dynamics: "Approximately 20% of small businesses fail within the first year, 33% of small businesses fail within two years. Roughly 50% of small businesses fail within five years, and 66% of small businesses fail within 10 years."[1]

These numbers speak for themselves on how staggeringly low the success rate is for owners surviving in business. If you look around at all the businesses in your current space or down the street, there is a high probability that only a small percentage of them will still be around ten years from now based on the statistics above. If it is true that 66 percent fail within ten years, then only 33 percent of entrepreneurs will actually succeed.

Honestly, when I see these numbers, I still don't believe it fully. Even if you are in the percentage of businesses that happen to make it for ten years, that doesn't mean you are

———

1   Michael T. Deane, "Top 6 Reasons New Businesses Fail," Investopedia, February 28, 2020.

successful or dominating your market, right? You may still be scraping by or paying yourself a minimal salary and have total gross sales under a million dollars. You see it all the time with mom-and-pop stores that are only working *in* their business instead of working *on* their business.

Based on my eighteen years of experience, I believe that out of the 33 percent of businesses that will actually make it to ten years, maybe one out of ten is actually a very successful entrepreneur and has financial freedom. These entrepreneurs have built a strong base with expansion mindsets and recurring income. These are the people who are truly successful and are building a legacy.

Granted, these numbers are on a typical year and not subject to any governmental changes, pandemics such as the one that is happening while writing this book, or any other external forces that we cannot control as business owners. Just as many successful entrepreneurs have managed to overcome these challenges, Ron Carson, founder of The Carson Group, has managed to defy these small business odds in his professional voyage.

Ron Carson's journey from starting a company with zero dollars in his college dorm room to building a company which manages over $15 billion in assets is an impeccable example of growing properly. His compelling story of dedication, innovation, and diversification is what all entrepreneurs dream and strive for.

Ron told me in an interview last year that when he was building his financial advisory company in Omaha, Nebraska, he understood that he had to stand out from the crowd and have a competitive advantage over other businesses in his industry. Even though he had built an extremely successful company and had become a Barron's Hall of Fame firm, he recognized that there was always room for improvement and innovation, especially with back-office technology. Ron realized that he could operate his organization more efficiently if it had the right technology. He needed a technology that would work hand in hand with his business model and a central platform to eliminate overlapping redundancies and create a stream-lined and seamless process for future growth.

After investigating the market and realizing there was nothing that would fit with Carson Wealth's structure and innovation, Ron invested heavily in research and development to create the perfect formula for the backbone of financial technology.

Once the technology was set in place, Ron's company began to reap the rewards, and soon it gained the attention of others in the industry. Ron began selling and implementing his software to hundreds of other firms that would also benefit from a strong infrastructure base. His proprietary technology helped financial firms with the latest technology, branding, marketing resources, investment strategies, compliance, and billing, just to name a few.

Soon Ron's company and software were well known in the financial-advisory marketplace. He realized how much of an impact he had on so many individuals. He then began training and coaching businessmen and businesswomen to succeed in their fields across North America.

Ron didn't simply grow his initial financial advisory company; he horizontally expanded it by creating other add-on services and opportunities that tied into his main solutions. This thought process of finding related industries and projects to build is what propelled Ron's business to what it has become today. I was curious if people like Ron were unique or part of a larger trend of entrepreneurs who treat their businesses differently by seeking out alternative collaborating opportunities. What I found is that a mindset of thinking horizontally when growing any business is the true key to success.

Most people believe in and are taught about vertical growth, which is the focus on one service or one product and selling that service as much as possible. Everyone thinks that to be a great entrepreneur you have to focus on growing vertically, growing your business as big as you can, gaining as much of the market share as you can, and pushing out all of your competitors. This mindset of gaining an incredible amount of clients works for some, but I'm here to tell you that it will never let you expand and grow enough to properly achieve your dreams. At some point it will plateau or even begin to decline over the course of time.

Another way to view vertical growth was outlined in an article by *FrogDog Magazine*, "When a company employs a vertical growth strategy, they take over a function previously held by a supplier. The organization grows by taking more control over their product or service." The article goes on to share that "Vertical growth is a compelling strategy for companies that have a strong competitive position within a popular industry. They are able to improve their competitive position by expanding along the value chain."[2]

The major problem with thinking this way is that you are allowing way too much risk by putting your focus on one avenue. Although this strategy may work for a small handful of entrepreneurs, it is so important to start thinking outside of the box. You must be willing to change your thought process on building your company so your growth does not plateau. To win at entrepreneurship, you have to find ways to expand your brand and stop focusing on growing one aspect of your company.

With the horizontal growth mentality, you still are keeping an eye on your main income source, but you are also always looking for corollary opportunities to build upon that main source. This means offering an array of products and services to your customers to create more sales, larger sales options and to provide your clients with something that they were previously purchasing from somewhere else. Once you have multiple products or services you are offering your clients, you can then focus on growing your overall organization to greater potentials.

FrogDog's article also shares this same logic to back up this ideology, "Companies that pursue a horizontal growth strategy expand their products or services into new markets, increasing the size of their target audience. Organizations

---

2   "Strategies for Growth," *FrogDog Magazine,* January 6, 2016.

can grow horizontally through internal development or externally through acquisitions or strategic alliances."[3]

It's like stacking blocks into one large tower. At some point it will get too tall and start to sway; it will eventually lose its support and crumble. However, if you were to build a bigger base or supporting structures around it, they will help to reinforce your initial structure and allow you to grow higher.

I am compelled to write this book about horizontal expansion to shed light on what I've learned from truly successful entrepreneurs and what they have built. As long as I can remember, I've had this mindset and thought process of expansion into complimenting products and services.

I remember starting my first business at nine years old selling golf balls to passing golfers behind my parents' home. Soon I added water and soda to the sales mix, helping build the foundation by consistently looking at what else I could offer my clients. From that moment on, I have built my four businesses in my adult years on the ideology that by utilizing current assets, staff, and clients, I can generate other sales sources to grow a structurally strong enterprise.

Since the early days of selling pop and golf balls, I took what I learned at age fifteen to start a lawn and landscape company that continues to currently grow year after year. The ability to shift into other businesses that complement the lawn and landscape industry has been a hobby of mine. Finding niches of corollary opportunities such as home renovations,

---

3   Ibid.

construction equipment manufacturing, and numerous other ventures is what drives me day after day to continue to build a legacy.

I once was focused solely on one service and one source of income in one of my first businesses, a lawn-care company. By putting all my focus on only growing mowing customers, I was losing out on rapid growth and rapid success. Instead, I experienced slow, methodical, and gradual growth. It took many years to understand and realize that by having blinders on with one service and not opening up my options to provide additional add-on products and services, my success was prolonged much longer than it should have been.

Since my first business venture, I have had the urge to create. I've had the focus to build companies and the drive to help people along the way. I've had many hurdles from where I came at nine years old, from lawsuits, staffing issues, monetary funding, and everything in between. By having gone through these hurdles, I was able to utilize the knowledge learned and build several successful companies that all complement each other. Each hurdle was and continues to be a learning advantage for business. I discovered what to do, what not to do, and how to expect these challenges before they even present themselves.

Today's most successful business owners and operators don't just look to grow. They seek out, brainstorm, and find opportunities to extend and expand their businesses through complementing avenues. So, whether you are a new business owner, someone aspiring to start your own company, an owner that feels stuck with the current level of business, or an operator in a managerial position, you will find many important principles and mindsets for expanding your company in the chapters ahead.

If you currently have problems with sales or performance becoming stagnant, this book will help you learn to identify new opportunities in your industry. You will be able to rise above and have a different perspective on your business and industry. Even if you haven't started any businesses yet, this book will help you identify what you should be looking for in diversification later down the road.

I believe that everyone has many strengths that separate each person from the masses, but there are two that truly make you who you are: your obsessions and your focus. These two characteristics are ways to maximize your goals and dreams to enhance and build your business. In the following chapter, we will go over how to utilize these to your advantage.

Throughout this book you will be shown a variety of different stories from successful individuals such as John Paul DeJoria, Nebraska natives Travis Freeman, Van Deeb, and Ron Carson, to name a few. All were able to break out of vertical thinking and into expansive, horizontal thinking. You will learn from business owners who took their already successful businesses and catapulted them to greatness by thinking horizontally. You will learn to expand quicker than ever before and create a business—or multiple businesses—that generate numerous streams of income. This key mindset will truly complement your current status and help you to achieve your financial freedom goal.

I truly believe that with the stories you will hear, along with my past experiences and insights, you can discover how to generate more revenue and create wealth!

1

HOW WE
GOT HERE

CHAPTER 1

OBSESSED AND FOCUSED ENTREPRENEURS

———

Can you remember a time when you felt so focused on a task that you lost track of time? When you wanted to keep pushing and keep working so that nothing could stand in your way or slow you down? Deep down, I seemed to have this feeling more times than not and was curious if this was a common trait. What I found is that this is a prevalent characteristic of successful people across all industries.

Studies by psychologist Mihály Csíkszentmihályi suggest this "flow state" is associated with subjective well-being, satisfaction with life and happiness, and in a business setting, is linked to motivation and productivity. Csíkszentmihályi defines this state as, "concentration that is so intense that no attention is left over to think about anything irrelevant or to worry about problems. Self-consciousness disappears, and the sense of time becomes distorted."[4]

During my youth, I was always obsessed with work. I loved it! Making that first dollar and my first paycheck working in a local bakery all gave me a sense of purpose and accomplishment. I was a sponge and wanted to absorb as much knowledge as I could about how businesses work and operate. Even then I displayed a focus and drive that made me who I am today: an entrepreneur who always wants to concentrate to improve my skills.

This perception of excitement creates a notion of comfort and the ability to work through any objective ahead of you. Maybe you've experienced this state during a sport you were participating in or while you were playing an instrument, but this heightened sense of focus and awareness is the main backbone to all successful entrepreneurs and provides the focus necessary to get through all tasks and stages of business.

The obsessive feeling to concentrate and create an opportunity runs through the veins of all successful people at an early age. Most don't realize where this comes from, but soon those small steps of achievement build into a larger base for their future endeavors.

I truly believe that there is a thought process that makes entrepreneurs obsessed with what they do. They are born to

---

4   Bryan Collins, "3 Surprising Benefits of Flow State," *Forbes*, March 31, 2020.

work hard and not to give up easily or without a fight. They will do whatever it takes to succeed and prosper.

For me and many other successful entrepreneurs, it starts with our first business and an obsessive focus on a main product or service. The beginning of my first legitimate business, a mowing business, started with mowing in my parents' neighborhood. I would go around and ask neighbors if I would be able to cut their grass for a small fee. My goal was to cut enough yards to not have to work for another person ever again. This focus and dedication began to gain traction and continued to grow throughout high school and college.

After many years of growth and adding in six other divisions of service for our clients, I was able to build a lawn and landscaping organization that services an entire metropolitan area and holds government contracts in five different states. Without the focus on being self-employed, I would not have been able to achieve the growth and success I desired.

Now my focus has shifted, becoming more analytical. I am constantly viewing and reviewing my lawn and landscape company as well as my other businesses, which include my real estate holding companies, a commercial real estate broker business, a construction equipment manufacturing company, a consulting service, and now two other companies that I have recently bought into. Each of these organizations I view as well-oiled machines, each with its own purpose and structure that contribute to my overall portfolio.

REMOVING YOURSELF, BOTH MIND AND BODY

One way that I became focused on my goals and companies was by elevating myself above the organization and always taking a look at all the moving parts. By separating and analyzing, you are able to constantly see what is working and what isn't working and also where possible opportunities are.

You must not lose focus on these moving parts otherwise one small gear may cause the entire company to lose traction and potentially fail. This focus will help identify any weaknesses so that you can then brainstorm possible solutions you can implement to turn that weakness into a strength. Each gear is a part of your machine: your employees, your operations, your marketing, your sales, and more. When one of these gears isn't working or not properly contributing to running your machine, the entire organization can suffer. These gears should be your key focus to view and manage.

With my current businesses, I am constantly thinking and brainstorming ideas. There's never a day or time that I am not thinking of what else I can be doing to reach a goal. Even while on vacation, I may be relaxed in a different city somewhere around the world, but in the back of my mind, the ideas never stop coming. When I am in a different city, state, or even country, my mind is removed from the day-to-day routine of normality. This allows me to concentrate on experiencing a different culture and somewhere along the way, the mind opens up to creative thinking. This is truly where I have found I am able to come up with unique ideas and audit all of my businesses.

If you are stuck and needing to create new ideas, I implore you to remove yourself from the day-to-day distractions of your business and do something that sets your mind at ease. Take a trip, go on a hike, or just get a hotel room where you can simply relax your mind. By taking your thoughts off your operations and business, you will come to find that some amazing ideas and processes will soon come into your mind.

One way to cultivate this passion is to seek out a company that is similar to yours in a different city or state. Call the owner and tell him or her you are going to be in town and would like to chat about their business and learn more about how they operate. Especially if you are in a different market, most business owners would gladly share their company's processes and operations with you. It will give you a chance to see a different perspective of how another individual has gained success.

Many things can be learned from an experience like this. By sharing both of your insights, it is a win-win for both parties, and hopefully you will walk away knowing more than when you began.

Several years back, I did this with a trip I had planned in Atlanta, Georgia, for a trade show. I knew I had an afternoon that was not filled yet and decided to reach out to a top landscaping company in the area. We went through their company and operations and went out to dinner to discuss more of the managerial processes as well. It was a great experience to learn how someone in a different part of the country operates and runs their company. I'm obsessed with learning as much about my companies' industries and want to gather as many insights as possible to form the best organization.

This simple task can break you out of your local market to see what others are doing within your industry or even similar industries. You have to always think about what new ideas and improvements you can bring to your company to succeed and one-up the competition.

I am constantly planning, thinking, and setting reminders with new ideas of what the next big thing will be. Thoughts on solving issues and implementing new processes are always noted as well. Whether it is during the day or in the middle of the night, it's a great way to keep track of thoughts and also stay organized.

This continual-thinking mindset is a blessing and a curse to all entrepreneurs. It gives us all the ability to create life-changing products and services for consumers, but at the same time, it keeps us from being able to fully relax. We often lack the ability to turn our brains off or be satisfied with a feeling of "just good enough."

This trait runs deep in my body, and I would never change this for anything. It has made me who I am today, and I know it will never change.

Most entrepreneurs believe that when they reach a certain milestone, they will become fulfilled. Perhaps the goal was making $100,000 a year. However, when it is reached, satisfaction is lacking. So much sweat, tears, time, and energy has been expended to reach this goal that one feels numb to the accomplishment. Visualizing it for so long and achieving it leaves you unimpressed with the result. Because it feels that not much has changed, you focus on the next milestone, which may be to have sales of $1,000,000.

The obsessed don't lose passion but just shift obsession to the next marker, the next goal, or the next big idea and do what it takes to create it.

FINDING INEFFICIENCIES

Not all obsessions deal with positive growth. Many successful entrepreneurs are also obsessed with failures. Having failures on your path to greatness allows you to learn new things and also brings out more forward thinking than if you did not have any failures. Billionaire, media magnate, and former executive chairman of both CBS and Viacom, Sumner Redstone, might as well speak for all successful entrepreneurs when he stated, "Great success is built on failure, frustration, even catastrophe."[5]

The more failures you have in business, the better you will become. I strongly believe that by working through these hurdles, you are more likely to attain higher success. You must remember that each failure or hurdle is a stepping-stone to something else and will eventually lead you to prosperity. This is why so many welcome and even obsess over failures, knowing that what they learn and how they grow after the failure will propel them to a better state of being.

---

5   "Sumner Redstone Quotes," Quotes Memo, accessed December 20, 2020.

Most failures are not catastrophic. They come in the form of small inefficiencies. However, these small inefficiencies may end up costing money and, if not taken care of, cause your business to suffer.

I'm always obsessed with looking for inefficiencies in every aspect of business. During the growth of my landscaping business, failures came in the form of not properly planning out processes and services, which inadvertently caused loss of efficiency and revenue. These mistakes can cost you thousands of dollars to correct if you fail to properly address them in the beginning stages.

In the earlier days of growing my business, we did not use GPS tracking on our service vehicles. We would constantly wonder why a certain crew was not completing their service stops in a timely fashion. It actually cost more to pay our employees on that crew than we were bringing in on sales by thousands of dollars. By focusing on the root of the inefficiency, we were able to brainstorm different options to enhance operations.

We began to put GPS tracking in all our vehicles and then analyzed the data. What we found was disturbing. In a ten-hour workday, some of the production crews were actually idling, driving, or stopping for breaks for over four hours every single day. The news was shocking! We quickly took administrative actions and were able to properly route and eliminate certain behaviors that were costing the company income.

By being focused on finding the inefficiencies in our company, we were able to cut loss of revenue and increase overall performance by implementing proper ethical work behavior and training.

Always focus—obsess even—on overcoming inefficiencies and failures. That mindset is why successful people such as John Paul DeJoria, founder of Paul Mitchell hair products, are never satisfied with "just good enough."

John Paul DeJoria has a truly rags-to-riches story. Growing up with a single mother of two, John and his brother wanted to support the family at a young age. Beginning when John was seven, he and his brother made and sold flowerpots and Christmas cards to anyone they could. They took most of their earnings and gave it to their mother so they could live a better life. John wasn't concerned with making money; he was just obsessed with work. [6]

Most entrepreneurs, including me, feel the same way as DeJoria. We are all obsessed with the flow state of working. I've grown up with the understanding that if you do the hard work first, the money will always follow.

DeJoria had many failures throughout his journey, and at one point in his life he was even homeless, but he never lost focus on his goal of becoming something great. He learned many insightful strategies and sales techniques during his time as

6   *Omar Elattar & The Passionate Few,* "How I Became a Billionaire After Being Broke & Homeless Twice (John Paul DeJoria Interview)," January 28, 2019, video, 53:53.

an encyclopedia salesperson and working with several hair product companies.

One quote DeJoria spoke stays with me every day. He stated, "You will knock on doors, and many will close on you. There will be people who don't like your product, your company— or you. To be successful, you must remain as confident and enthusiastic on door No. 59 as you were on door No. 1."[7] It is very important you realize this from the day you launch your business.

His obsession to continue to learn and grow his mind eventually allowed him to start John Paul Mitchell Systems with his friend Paul Mitchell in 1980 with only $700. John would not have had the ability to start this company without the steppingstones of knowledge and determination gained from his past employments and challenging times.[8]

DeJoria's true obsession was to create the finest products with Paul Mitchell. By implementing components such as using the best plants and ingredients, Paul Mitchell continues to provide the best products to consumers. From the day they started they were the first company to never test on animals, and they never will. John's obsession with creating the best salon-grade products helped the company to be the most well-known hair product company throughout eighty countries. If he had not had the continual obsession to give the highest quality and best product on the market, Paul

---

7 Ibid. 4:47.

8 Alexander Koerner, "John Paul DeJoria's Journey from Homeless to Billionaire," *NBC News*, May 30, 2018.

Mitchell definitely would not be the company we know and love today.[9]

With his continued obsession of providing the best products to consumers, he later co-founded Patrón Tequila. By focusing on every aspect of his businesses and processes, he ultimately created the perfect product. He found his flow state and was able to utilize his drive for finding and implementing the best ingredients, packaging, and processes to create the largest grossing premium tequila in the world. DeJoria's eye for quality in his product paid dividends when he recently sold Patrón in 2018 for $5.3 billion.[10]

His giant thinking soon spread to many other businesses and nonprofits as well, such as night clubs, other liquor companies, oil, solar, and natural gas, and mobile tech. Had he not become focused at an early age to think right and work hard, he would not have the legacy he has created today.

Similarly to John Paul DeJoria's focus on creating top-notch products, my good friends Kim and Jill Wolfe had a similar experience as they ensured they created the perfect medical transport business in the Midwest. They obsessed over the different ways they could outperform and out service the competition when they first founded Midwest Medical Transportation.

---

9   *Omar Elattar & The Passionate Few,* "How I Became a Billionaire After Being Broke & Homeless Twice (John Paul DeJoria Interview)," January 28, 2019, video, 53:53.

10   Ibid. 25:25.

When starting their business, they focused on making sure they would stand out from other national medical transport companies. The Wolfes focused on what they could do to ensure their services would rise above the competition to inevitably promote healthy growth. They provided the cleanest, newest, and most advanced ambulances, helicopters, and equipment above all their competition, which in turn created one of the best work environments for their growing staff.

What started with one ambulance in the small town of Columbus, Nebraska, soon began to gain traction throughout the state and transformed into a large and successful company. They always had the obsession to give back and do better for the customer and their communities. By having that mindset, Kim and Jill were able to implement unique ideas into an industry that previously did not exist.

Kim recently told me, "We used to think outside the box. What can we do to differentiate us from everyone else? In our ambulances, we thought about what we could do about patients in the back of the ambulances. They were feeling every bump in the road or wondering whether they were going to live or die. So we put DVD players up on the ceiling, and every company thought we were nuts because we gave them something to put them at ease."

By offering this simple idea to their patients being transported, they were able to calm their patients being transported to a different city. They wanted to focus on their client—the patient—and make their experience as enjoyable as it could be under the circumstances. Without thinking outside the box and having a deep care for their customers, they would not have had the success they achieved with their clients.

An obsessed entrepreneur needs to first focus on what his industry is missing or what he can improve upon to better serve customers. What would help make your industry more efficient? What can help your clients be better serviced? Once you have figured that out, you can provide the absolute best product and service to fill that gap, a service so great that it will leave a lasting positive impression in clients' minds, just as John Paul DeJoria and Kim and Jill Wolfe have done. Let's face it, if you have sub-par products or service, why would anyone want to do business with you or refer you to their family and friends? You need to establish an obsession and focus on what can set you apart from the competition.

No matter at what stage of business you currently are, you must train yourself in intensive, deep focus and finding your flow state. Eliminate clutter from your thoughts and dive fully into what is actually happening in your company. To be able to dominate your market space, you have to be obsessed with your organization and how you can improve and rise above the competition. By understanding and building on your obsession, you can focus on building your brand to best represent you. You are the key to the business, and in order to achieve greatness, you should make it a top priority to express your obsessive passion to your customers.

At the end of each chapter, I will be providing exercises to better help build your business. These questions and your answers should be revisited throughout the year to encourage your continual growth mentality.

Complete the exercise below to help you realize your obsession and how it can help you improve your business:

1. Write down what you are currently obsessed about or focused on.
2. How can you implement this focus and obsession toward your business, future business growth, or current sales period?
3. Who is somebody that you personally know that is obsessed?
4. What makes them that way, and what makes them want to succeed?

CHAPTER 2

SCIENCE OF DIVERSIFICATION

"Diversification is a protection against ignorance," according to Warren Buffett. "It makes very little sense for those who know what they're doing."[11]

In today's business world, the smart entrepreneur is always looking horizontally at building their business to diversify and create new sources of income. This isn't a new idea at all. Many well-known individuals have and continue to follow this process.

However, Warren's take on diversification is something that most don't realize. Without diversifying and creating multiple sources of income, not only do you reduce your overall risk, you are able to hedge your future with the best possible outcome with multiple options of income streams.

---

11 Karl Kaufman, "Here's Why Warren Buffett and Other Great Investors Don't Diversify," *Forbes,* July 24, 2018.

So what does diversification have to do with risk? Let's say you have one business and something catastrophic happens within your organization, your city, or your industry. Such catastrophes as a lawsuit, a new government policy, or even a natural disaster can quickly cripple your business. With only one source of income, your overall net worth will most likely suffer a major blow if anything were to happen.

Now, by diversifying into at least one other business or complimenting industry, you are cutting your risk in half. You are able to play the odds and have additional insurance against anything that may affect one of your businesses, thus limiting your overall risk.

Hiscox's DNA of an entrepreneur report, released in 2017, found that many entrepreneurs are juggling multiple businesses. In fact, approximately 26 percent of US small business owners surveyed are currently running more than one organization.[12]

People like Warren Buffett continuously look at following this concept for new opportunities and ideas that can spread out the risk of his empire. Warren is one of the most known icons of diversifying. At the time of writing this book, Buffett has over sixty companies under his ownership. His ability to see outside the box and create risk aversion makes him one of the greatest business owners in our history.

---

12 "The 2017 DNA of an Entrepreneur Report," *Hiscox* (blog), September 12, 2017.

Most of us may never reach the platform that Warren Buffett stands on, however, if it helped him to create a net worth of almost $80 billion, then he must be doing something right, and we can benefit from learning from his process.

By focusing on horizontal growth instead of vertical growth, you too can soon be on the same path as Buffett. It's time to start thinking of ways to expand your business or businesses—horizontal growth—and not focus on one product or service—vertical growth. You can break the traditional ways of thinking in building your empire and create a more stabilized portfolio.

USE CASH FLOW WISELY

I've had the pleasure of meeting and learning from sales guru and real estate mogul Grant Cardone about the science of diversification.

Grant preaches, "You want to find one or two spaces you completely understand that can't be destroyed and go all in. That's how people get rich. People don't get rich by tip-toeing in with $100 investments all over the place."

Don't get me wrong, diversification is a great tool, but there is a limit to how quickly and how methodically you should actually diversify.

Most people think that you should spread your money and time across as many things as possible. And for some, that may work. But for the majority of entrepreneurs, this is a dangerous and energy-draining theory. As we go through this book, we will discuss the science of smart diversification and its two components: creating additional cash-flow options in an industry with which you are already familiar and knowledgeable and focusing on what you are currently good at and building upon your main business.

The term diversification is defined by its root term "diverse," which is defined as "showing a great deal of variety." It goes on to further mean, "the process of a business enlarging or varying its range of products or field of operation."[13]

When implementing diversification, think of a basket of eggs as your main business income source. You want to ensure that it is getting most of your focus and attention to grow and scale into a larger, successful company. However, no one said you can't get a bigger basket, right? Once your main basket—business—is full of success and income, you can increase the size of your basket to include multiple different types of products or services— the eggs—that all will contribute to the basket you currently have.

Another form of diversification argues that by focusing on what you are good at and where the industry needs are, you can attain unlimited success. The science of diversification has worked for many people. There is never a right or wrong method to this mindset either, as I am still learning and growing each year as well. And year after year, I realize a new or more efficient way to spread out my risk and create new avenues of income. By looking around to other successful entrepreneurs, you will see that almost all of them have

---

13   *Lexico Online.* s.v. "Diverse (adj.)," accessed December 21, 2020.

diversified well and most likely have multiple businesses and streams of income. You too will discover how to create these other avenues throughout the next few chapters in this book.

FOCUS ON WHAT YOU ALREADY KNOW AND ARE GOOD AT

Recently, I have had the privilege to invest in other companies that were different baskets, to say the least. One is a bourbon-barrel-aged coffee company in addition to a tech-based employment startup. Both are owned by close friends of mine. Although this didn't tie directly to my main businesses of lawn, landscaping, or real estate, I was brought into these companies to help with scaling, financial, and operational processes, all with which I have over eighteen years of experience.

Despite the fact that I know nothing about aging and roasting coffee or the background of employment placing, I knew that these individuals came to me based on my successful reputation to build companies. I was not planning on being the CEO or majority owner of either of these companies, so by implementing my ideas and coaching to build these businesses, I knew there was opportunity to create something successful.

Even though my main focus is with my current companies and ensuring proper and healthy growth, I always look for other diversifying opportunities. As long as I have a professional attribute to offer and provide in hopes of creating additional revenue and overall net worth, then I can help others and also benefit from the diversification venture benefits.

No matter what your business is, there are options to expand your existing business with horizontal diversification through different products, services, and corollary businesses. We will discuss this ideology of corollaries in "Chapter 4—Looking for Corollaries."

DIVERSIFY CLIENTELE AND CUSTOMER BASE, NOT JUST BUSINESS OPPORTUNITIES

My uncle-in-law, Achim Romanowski, built a very well-known architecture firm in Germany. Romanowski Architects provides a unique streamlined process from the design process through construction phases. Originally there were only architects, and then there were only construction companies, but Achim found a way to combine both under his management and create the successful company he has today. Having contracts with local municipalities, private firms, and the United States military, his high quality of work and service made him very well renowned in the area.

During his company's growth, he was faced with a major hurdle. Fifteen years ago, Achim had over twenty employees working in Manheim, Germany, at the US installation. Without notice, the US government decided to close the installation overnight. The contracts were canceled, and per German law, he would have to pay all the employees one to two months' salary after letting them go.

With this one major speedbump, Achim thought it was all over. No one was going to help him during those stressful and sleepless nights ahead of him. It was up to him to problem solve and be strong enough to win. He had to adapt, he had to think, and he had to do it quickly.

After brainstorming and weighing options in his mind, Achim shifted his thought process and started looking for different opportunities to diversify his services and customer base. He eventually found new work and contracts in a different town and moved all of his employees that were currently in working limbo. He was able to keep all of the employees staffed and in turn had a better contract for future revenue by not focusing all his attention on only a few larger contracts.

This one obstacle created an important thought process that would be used for all of Achim's future planning. Instead of having 70–80 percent of his sales with the US government exclusively, he was able to adapt and diversify with a wide array of clients and government agencies. If this issue arose again with one of his projects, it wouldn't cause much effect on his revenue or staff.

My uncle did not go over the hurdles but instead went in another direction to avoid them altogether. By having multiple streams of income and client bases, the chances of losing revenue diminishes. You create well-balanced income streams and are able to adapt and overcome any shortcomings.

Achim's business and your business can diversify in a variety of different ways. You can diversify with the different types of businesses or services you can offer, or you can diversify with your client base. Both are very important to incorporate and will inevitably help spread out risk and also increase wealth.

Just like my uncle's company, I too was able to implement client-based diversification for my lawn and landscape company. I realized there was more business available than just selling our service to homeowners. I was always looking for the next challenge and would learn the process of gaining traction in different markets. In college, I worked closely with our local business development association to become certified and qualified to bid and eventually be awarded multiple government contracts that included city and military grounds maintenance. Soon those contracts spread into five different states and through various government agencies.

Throughout the growth of one of my companies which focuses on year-round lawn and landscape services, I realized the significance of this thought process and its importance during the beginning years. We always had a goal to have a well-rounded client base which was constructed by different commercial properties, municipalities, and residential clients.

A good goal that should be implemented into your business as well is to never have one client make up more than 10–15 percent of your overall sales.

This is a great way to ensure that if something was to happen to that client, your business would still be able to operate without a major hit to the bottom line. This 10 percent rule, as I like to call it, is another way to move the hurdles altogether from your future growth and horizontally diversify properly.

During the pandemic outbreak of COVID-19 in 2020, we recently lost some of our contracts with larger hotel chains and retail stores. These companies were forced to shut down business operations across the nation. It goes to show how things can change quickly, even when you are providing top-notch services, and there is nothing you can do about it. Although these contracts only made up a small percentage of our total sales, it was still lost income. However, because of our diversification and the 10 percent rule, we were easily able to continue and gain more clients to fill those voids within a matter of days.

I wasn't getting hung up wondering why this was happening to us or how much money we were going to lose. Instead, we instantly shifted gears, cranked up our marketing budget, and gained far more business than what we had lost. Let's say the percentages were different, however, and those contracts made up 40 percent of our overall revenue. Do you think it would impact and most likely cause a business to make drastic changes and possibly close? You're damn right it would.

I know plenty of companies in my industry that don't diversify properly. If they only had large contracts with the hospitality or restaurant industries, they would have been severely impacted by the extended government shutdown of the economy during this pandemic.

For most, there is no recovering from catastrophic events, and only those that truly know how to diversify will weather those storms. It has happened in the past, and I'm certain unexpected circumstances will happen again in the future.

I see so many people and businesses that rely on a few clients for all of their sales. Honestly, this scares the heck out of me. Whether they only provide their product to one retailer or only have a handful of clients they provide their services to, this is a nightmare waiting to happen. You need to sit down and truly think cynically for a moment. Think about all the crippling things that could happen. Maybe that retailer hires a new CEO and changes the direction of their purchasing, or maybe the company goes bankrupt. What if the supply chain is affected getting your product to their store? There could also be a natural disaster or economic pandemic during which that client won't be able to open for months on end.

Most business gurus will say that you have to always be positive and optimistic as an entrepreneur. However, when it comes to business, you must still think of what the worst-case scenarios can also be. By coming up with all the possible issues that may arise beforehand, you have an advantage to start planning ahead and diversifying to reduce risk before anything could happen.

Always think about new opportunities with this mindset. Times and technology are constantly changing around us, and we must constantly seek out new ideas and ways to eliminate risk. Picture this like surfing a large wave; you can either paddle toward it and ride it, or you are going to be swept up in the undertow and crushed.

I recommend doing an exercise of writing down all the threats against your business and clients several times a year, either by yourself or with your management team. Then next to each threat, list possible ways to hedge against them or minimize any major losses. This will keep your mind thinking how you can continue to seek out new business and what you can do to expand your organization. You will find new opportunities and sales avenues just by completing this simple exercise. Write down every idea that comes to mind, and then weigh each opportunity based on plausibility. The more people you can reach and sell to, the better you will be moving forward to prevent any major downshifts in sales.

Although this is only one aspect in business you will face as an entrepreneur, this is one of the biggest that typically gets overlooked. The worst thing you can do is start to feel content and happy where you are with your business. It is usually this point in time when something disastrous can occur and pull you down into the undertow of the wave.

Diversify in your field, seek out new opportunities, and never stop creating new ideas.

Exercise:

1. What sets your company apart from your competitors? How can you can capitalize upon this?
2. What traits do you possess for which you can find other avenues to diversify?

3. Create a breakdown of all clients as a percentage of total sales. Are any more than 10 percent? If so, you need to look at diversifying your clientele to avoid any major issues that may arise.
4. What internal and external threats may affect your business or clients? What can you do to minimize any major downfalls?

CHAPTER 3

IMPORTANCE NOW: SPEED OF CHANGE

Most people on this earth hear their alarm clock go off every morning and dread the day ahead of them. They wish their life were better and hope that something magical would happen in their day-to-day routine that would make them miraculously become rich and allow them to be truly happy.

When recently discussing daily morning routines with Ron Carson, founder of The Carson Group, he mentioned something that will forever stick in my mind. Ron said, "If you start hitting the snooze button on your phone or alarm clock more than a few times, that's an early warning sign of cancer on your enthusiasm."

Ron went on to say, "Either you're getting depressed, or it's something else. A lot of times we start feeling down and not even sure why. And I would argue most every time, it's because you're not living a purpose-filled life, which you're just on this unconscious journey to arrive at death safely.

That's no way to live. You know you want to get to the end and say 'I'm glad I did,' and not 'I wish I had done something more.'"

I never really thought about this, but it is remarkably accurate. Life is your alarm clock, and the more you push snooze, the more you are delaying your talent and your opportunities to gain horizontal growth. You have to recognize that there is no better time than now to change and implement procedures to set yourself up for future success.

I'm not going to lie, there have been many times that I have hit the snooze on my alarm more than once or twice. I recently thought of Ron when I was doing this in bed as well. I had to think to myself, "Why in the heck am I pushing the snooze button? I have a new day to kick ass!" Was it because I went to bed too late? Was it because there was a major issue at work that had to be confronted the next day? Or was it merely that I was losing enthusiasm?

I kept coming back to the main reason of simply not being fully rested or having a racing mind. I tend to get up throughout the night thinking about all the goals and objectives I have currently at hand or what needs to be accomplished for the upcoming day. I also try to wake up at a minimum two to three hours before my office opens just so I can fully run through my day and plan everything out when there is a calm and collected time in the morning. I wish I was one of those individuals that wakes up without any alarm clock. However, I feel that I exert myself from sunrise to far past sundown most nights and become physically and emotionally drained.

This isn't a bad thing at all though! Knowing that I am trying to utilize as much of my day as possible truly gives me more energy and allows me to continue reaching my goals with horizontal development.

This feat would be much more difficult if I had a wife or kids. I would not be able to put as much effort and time into my businesses and still keep my family life healthy. So for that, I am fortunate to be able to build as much as I can now, fully knowing that down the line when I have my future family, I will be able to provide and spend more time with them doing the things we love.

This is my now-or-never theory and my personal "Why?" that gives me confidence and enthusiasm to live every moment of every day. I want to build an empire now through horizontal growth, not wait for someone else to build it while I watch from the sidelines, not wait until I am older and wish I could have, should have, or would have. Time is the one thing we can't get back, and I want to make sure it is being utilized to its fullest extent while on this earth. I want to ensure that my family will be provided for and create a legacy that can be passed down to my kids' kids.

MINDSET TO MAKE THE CHANGE TO NOW

Matt Mayberry, CEO of Matt Mayberry Enterprises, shared his insights in *Entrepreneur* magazine for making the change to now philosophy. Matt went on to claim, "It's important to approach each assignment, task and project with extreme care and focus, but being a perfectionist often hinders the sense of urgency needed to produce. Whether it is letting your perfectionism slow your growth or waiting for the perfect moment rather than creating a sense of urgency to make it happen and get it done, you must be deliberate in your efforts to identify a sense of urgency in all that you do."[14]

I believe most entrepreneurs see themselves as perfectionists, even myself. According to what Matt claimed above, I know this is a hindering trait that can slow us down. We need to put this characteristic aside and truly understand that now is the best time to act and do so now before it is too late.

If you are still wondering how to create this sense of urgency, I'm going to tell you now that there is no magic eight ball or genie that will help you except you. If you aren't happy with your life, you need to take a step back and start figuring out why that is. Are you unhappy being around coworkers? Does your boss not treat you professionally or belittle you? Are you pursuing your wrong passion? Or is it something completely outside of work that is affecting your life?

I know plenty of people, and even past employees, that complained about not being happy because they don't make enough money, yet the money they're making isn't really the issue. Instead of planning properly and being money smart, they are spending money at the bar five or more times a week, buying drugs, or spontaneously purchasing things that will not advance them in life.

---

14   Matt Mayberry, "Don't Lose That All-Important Sense of Urgency. Do It—Now!," *Entrepreneur*, May 14, 2016.

It's tough. I get it, and I have been there. I've spent money I didn't have in college and bought thousands of dollars of things that I did not need. But there is a chance for you to change your path forward and start your change of mindset.

If you haven't started your journey yet, now is the time. You can easily change your mindset to achieve horizontal growth no matter at what stage in life you are.

W. Clement Stone, the late, great businessman, philanthropist, and author, had a success statement that he thought was one of the most powerful statements you could ever say to yourself: "Do it now."[15]

No matter how rough life seems right now, many successful individuals have experienced similar situations. It can be done if you get your mind right and make the change. Never think it's too late or you missed your chance.

One of the best examples of a successful entrepreneur is that of Colonel Harland Sanders. Harland had one of the roughest lives before creating what we know today as Kentucky Fried Chicken.

---

15   Ibid.

At the age of six years old, his father passed away, and at twelve, his mother remarried to a man who would abuse Harland. After marrying his wife, Harland's only son died at an early age. Not too long after, while Harland was on a business trip, his wife sold all their belongings and left with their two daughters.[16]

Sanders then spent twenty-five years in the restaurant business creating his signature recipe we know today but eventually went broke at age sixty five. He ended up living in his car, traveling around the country for two years looking for someone to purchase his specialty recipe.[17]

Not only did he face objection a few times, he was rejected 1,009 times before finally finding a restaurant that would agree to use his recipe. Nine years after he started traveling the country broke and homeless, Sanders had 600 franchises selling his trademarked chicken.[18]

Colonel Sanders could have been satisfied with one restaurant and lived comfortably. However, he thought about horizontal growth and diversifying into other cities, other states, and other countries. Can you imagine if he didn't have the passion to build and grow rapidly? He recognized the urgency to spread his product onto as many kitchen tables as possible, and in doing so, created a very successful household name.

---

16   Chris Heasman, "The Tragic, Real-Life Story of Colonel Sanders," *Mashed*, August 12, 2018.

17   Dennis Nafte, "Colonel Sanders Failed 1009 Times Before Succeeding," *Medium*, September 10, 2017.

18   Ibid.

According to *Forbes*, the brand is valued at $8.3 billion and ranks 96th on their World's Most Valuable Brands 2020 list.[19]

No matter what your age is or the struggles you are currently battling, experiencing change can be important. As long as you have the want and the desire, no one can take your drive away from you.

You have a lifetime of opportunities at your fingertips, and the only one keeping you from achieving greatness is yourself.

You must break through the chains that are pulling you back each day and make it your most productive day yet. There is no better time than now to start building and creating.

If you currently are an entrepreneur and have a steady or even a successful business, never waste any days to achieve your goals. Opportunity awaits around each corner if you know where to look and where to focus your attention.

You will never attain horizontal growth unless you begin now. It's time to push out the negative thoughts and procrastination from your brain and start thinking about how you can implement changes into your current company.

---

19   Marty Swant, "The World's Most Valuable Brands," *Forbes,* Accessed January 16, 2021.

The willingness to do better and create more should be on your daily agenda, your monthly, quarterly, and yearly benchmarks. Without jumping in and starting today, you will end up pushing the snooze button on your dreams until it is too late and you wake up realizing and wishing you would have done something sooner.

I don't want to limit your expectations, but it is highly unlikely that tomorrow you will create a million dollars and your life will miraculously change. You need to start looking at all opportunities that will move you forward and create openings for growth.

My uncle Achim Romanowski, who is a successful business owner of an architectural firm in Germany, articulated this concept impeccably when he told me recently about his view on the speed of acting now, "One dollar is just as important as $1 million. Each project and each sale are very important. If I take the smaller projects, I will get the larger projects. Always look at the smaller sums, and the bigger sums will come and will bring larger ideas which you can capitalize on."

There is no such thing as negative growth. Each idea and each sale teach you something on your path to greater opportunity and success. Without starting off with the smaller sales, you will not be ready to take a stab at the colossal opportunities. You have to start somewhere to begin to learn all the ins and outs of each avenue you pursue. The amount of knowledge and corollary opportunities you experience by taking small action will greatly impact your life and your business.

Take a step back and think about where you want to be in life. There are plenty of opportunities out there waiting for you to capitalize on. These opportunities should tie into your personal wants and needs and help to build your empire. Take the initiative to change your mindset today and dive into what you truly want, what you believe in, and what will positively change your future.

Exercise:

1. List three indicators that you believe are inhibiting your creative and adventurous mindset.
2. Write down why you are wanting to create a better future and legacy. Is it your wife, kids, community, etc.?
3. What are three ambitions that you have wanted to accomplish but have been putting off?
4. What steps, objectives, or projects can you do now to start the snowball effect to success?

2

PRINCIPLES OF THE EXPANSION MINDSET

CHAPTER 4

LOOKING FOR COROLLARIES

———

"Companies that grow for the sake of growth or that expand into areas outside their core business strategy often stumble. On the other hand, companies that build scale for the benefit of their customers and shareholders more often succeed over time."[20]

– *JAMIE DIMON, PRESIDENT AND CEO OF JPMORGAN CHASE*

This quote is a kinder way of saying not to be selfish. Stop thinking of yourself, and your business will flourish.

Rise above the masses of mediocre thinking and truly feel the need to help people!

———

20 Shalini Nagarajan, "'The Market Doesn't Care Who You Are:' 11 of JPMorgan CEO Jamie Dimon's Best Quotes," *Business Insider,* June 17, 2020.

Jamie Dimon's point of expansion for the right reasons is what you and your company should be focusing on. There is no other option to grow other than focusing on a way to benefit your customers and employees. If you create that benefit and that want for your clients, the horizontal growth will come naturally and without pressure. You must listen to what your clients are asking for and what void in their relationship with your business that you can fill with a high quality product or service.

You must think about the Five P's when considering growth: Proper planning prevents poor performance.

By researching and planning your corollary growth potential, you eliminate any poor performance or failures with expansion.

So how can you figure out what your corollaries are to grow horizontally? What the heck does a corollary even mean?

We will examine two types of corollaries. The first example is the products or services that may be offered to your clients that complement what they have currently purchased from you. These can be a variety of different small or large ticket items that can easily be added onto the original sale. This can also be offered as a cross-sell into a different product altogether to offer more benefit to the client.

When I started my first business in high school, I was offering mowing services to my parents' neighbors. I continued to grow and provide the best service that I could. It wasn't too much further down the road when clients started to ask me if I did other services such as landscape maintenance, fertilizing, snow removal, and more. For a while, I would decline and inform them that it was outside of my wheelhouse. However, as time went on, I knew that if I would be able to learn that service, it would bring in a new stream of sales revenue, in addition to the current service I was providing.

I soon began to offer complementing corollaries such as fertilizing and landscape maintenance while we were already on site at their property. It was an easy add-on service to accompany mowing services. Soon, we would offer larger ticket corollaries such as renovating their entire landscaping or installing a sprinkler system. By being able to offer the client a one-stop shop, we were able to dramatically grow the business and increase our bottom line.

Fast forward several years: I had taken this mindset and would continue to build different divisions to better serve our clients. I would learn and master new services such as sprinkler service work, holiday lighting, and much more. We would continue to provide those services to build up sales until that division was mastered and was self-sustaining with income and growth. At a specific point when the right number of sales were coming in and creating more revenue, I would seek out a skilled professional with that background and bring them on board to run and grow that service division.

It was quite the process with many growing pains and headaches trying to figure out new corollary services to provide our clients. Many worked, and some did not. By reviewing performance indicators, we were able to keep and expand on the services that provided the best net income and scrap the ones that had too low of margins. At the time of writing this book, what started as a one-service business now has seven different divisions, which each offer a wide array of products and services within that division title to our clients.

By embracing the corollary mindset, our lawn and landscape company grew from a summer-time hobby to a multi-million-dollar operation that continues to grow into new markets every year.

Another perk of having corollary options occurs when a new customer signs up with the intention of only having one service done then quickly realizes that we can take care of all their needs under one roof.

The ability to easily cross sell and offer multiple services catered to the client is one of the best ways to ensure you will have lower overall risk in your organization and maintain positive corollary growth.

Investigate and realize what your customers are already purchasing and acquiring from other companies. By taking this data and analyzing it, you will be able to see if that is something you can offer to bring their business to you. People like simplification and would rather spend money in one place where it is most easy for them with the best overall performance benefit. This idea of the second sale is one of the easiest ways to increase your income.

This process is not only beneficial to our company, but it also creates an easier process for our clients to deal with only one service provider to take care of all their needs. Where previously they may have had anywhere from three to seven different contractors, we are making our clients' lives easier in turn; this benefits both parties.

You can also create a new opportunity that maybe your customer doesn't currently have anyone providing to them. This route still takes observing and investigating ways to enhance your clients' overall goals with your company. If something will make them feel better and enhance their lives, they will most likely be willing to spend extra for that product or service.

I was recently having breakfast with Travis Freeman, a good friend and mentor of mine. He had a similar experience with his lawn care company back in the '80s and '90s. One winter, he had bought lots of equipment to perform snow-removal services for his clients. However, that year there was not much snow, and the equipment was not being utilized or generating any income. He began to talk to clients and found that there were people who wanted help installing their Christmas lights on their homes. Since there was not much other income coming in during the months leading up to Christmas, he started offering this service to his existing customers.

Travis quickly realized that there was an untapped market for this service. He soon also realized that the products sold at the local home stores were not very unique for people wanting to stand out and create a much more elaborate lighting display. With metal, lights, and tape, he started making decorative holiday lights in his parent's basement and garage, which would inevitably be his "linkable" lighting product. These products were made in an array of different colors and shapes such as snowflakes, icicles, stockings, and more. His product rapidly got attention in the market, and soon he couldn't keep up with the demand for his unique lighting products. He even had to reach out to other local contractors in the area and share his idea to help them create an alternative income too.

What started as an alternative avenue to generate money when times were slow quickly grew into one of the largest holiday lighting companies in the US. During his growth, clients would often ask Travis to ship his products out of state because of the uniqueness and quality of product. Travis quickly thought, "If we are having this much growth in one city, how can we duplicate our processes in different cities across the states?" With this thought process, he quickly began offering distributor licenses across North America and now has over 500 preferred distributors purchasing and installing his products. Brite Ideas Decorating continues to create state-of-the-art lighting options for not just Christmas but for an array of holidays throughout the year.

His adaptation to look for corollaries during difficult times actually provided an opportunity for a new service and industry need that superseded his original business many times over. Even after creating this new revolutionary industry, there were many corollary products that Travis was able to capitalize upon with his holiday lighting customers to bring in additional sales avenues, such as interior decor and home goods.

I love and admire Travis' passion for finding alternative routes of creating income-producing products and services and unique opportunities that can shake an industry altogether.

> During times of hardship, you often find new ideas, new sales avenues, and new corollaries that can propel your business to success.

FINDING COROLLARY PRODUCTS

Even if you are not in the service-related industry, there are still plenty of ideas to find related corollaries. Endless amounts of opportunities exist to create unique packages or promotional products. You must think about what other products you can add to your arsenal that will intrigue and benefit your clients.

For example, let's say you have a coffee business that offers a wide array of drinks to your patrons. What other ideas would work hand in hand with the main products you are selling? How about pastries, breakfast snacks, or drinkware?

Starbucks did a great job at this by thinking about what else their consumers wanted. They knew that once their consumer decided to come in for coffee and make that initial purchase, there was a much higher probability they would be willing to add something else on to that sale.

By realizing the corollaries that their customers were interested in and most likely purchasing elsewhere, they began to offer additional products to their customers outside of their cup of coffee. They began selling muffins, scones, whole coffee bags of beans, thermoses, and much more. Their marketing and product placements inside each of their stores brought attention to these product corollaries. When a customer would go in to only purchase a cup of coffee, they would see the additional add-on products, which in turn increased the chances of spending more money in their store.

According to Starbucks' annual report, in 2019 the company had just over $10.5 billion in sales from food, packaged material, and other merchandise only.[21] Yes, that is billion with a "B" in sales of add-on, corollary products. This number does not include the sale of the coffee products we all know and love.

Let's break down and put into perspective Starbucks' corollary sales. Did you know that a country located in the South Pacific called Tuvalu has a GDP (gross domestic product)

---

21   "Starbucks Fiscal 2019 Annual Report," *Starbucks Corporation,* Accessed December 14, 2020.

that was only approximately $53 million in 2019?[22] In comparison, Starbucks' corollary products will surpass Tuvalu's GDP by the second day of the year! Can you imagine if they didn't add these product lines to complement their coffee drinks? That is crazy! By coming up with additional corollary products to provide to customers, Starbucks actually created more revenue than the GDP of forty seven countries in the world.[23] To say the least, I don't believe Starbucks will be reducing their product lineups any time soon.

As you are reading this book, you must be wondering how you can mirror Starbucks' or Travis Freeman's successes. First you must focus on your main product or service. One of my favorite quotes from John Paul DeJoria was what he attributed to all his success, "You are in the re-order business and your product must be the best on the market."[24]

One thing I hear from many companies is that they are only concerned with the initial sale. They don't think about the re-order. Without wrapping your mind around how you can truly be the best in your industry by having customers continue to re-order your products and services, you will never reach a successful state of business.

22 "GDP Ranked by County 2020," *World Population Review,* Accessed January 17, 2021.

23 Ibid.

24 *Omar Elattar & The Passionate Few,* "How I Became a Billionaire After Being Broke & Homeless Twice (John Paul DeJoria Interview)," January 28, 2019, video, 53:53.

Anyone can make a sale, but those that continue to sell to the same clients are what separates the ordinaries from the greats.

Above all, your product or service must be of quality in order for your customers to want to re-order. You must differentiate yourself from the competition in order to keep your clients coming back. Those that utilize this advice will not only see an increase in sales, they will also have a much more sustainable company with a higher valuation over time.

By actually listening to your clients and figuring out accompanying products and services that will better their lives, you will be able to spread your income out over different avenues. Even if you don't come up with the next best idea or revolutionary product, there are still simple opportunities that can turn into great sales successes.

Some products and services that you add on to your list may not realize the profit margins you anticipated. It would be best to scrap them. It may be beneficial to contract out that process to reduce overhead and risk. By contracting out the production or service all together, you are able to still generate some revenue without all the headaches of keeping it in house.

We will discuss in a later chapter how to analyze and determine the proper strategy of selecting and managing corollary options.

IDENTIFYING EXTERNAL COROLLARIES

Another example of corollaries is based on a broader view of your company, the larger perspective that allows you to not only look within your organization but to take a step back and observe from an external view point. This form of corollary can be a new business or new idea that you can start up and offer to existing clients through an entirely different venture. There can also be corollary businesses that simply make your company more efficient.

Let's look at a few examples of how this type of corollary can be implemented.

For one of my companies, Elkhorn Lawn Care, we always had a lull in sales in the winter months compared to the summer months, and that made it difficult to keep employees productive year-round. Even with holiday lighting and snow removal services, we could not maximize our abilities throughout the winters. Many years ago, we would brainstorm about what other opportunities we could create in order to keep paying our staff and also grow their interest in our future growth vision.

We began to write down current assets, equipment, and the skills of our team members. Once we had this data, we were able to come up with ideas that would benefit not only the employees but also provide additional growth to my overall business portfolio. What we came up with was to start another entity altogether that would purchase and renovate single-family homes that we could turn into rental properties or flip for sale based off the project.

The great thing about renovating and single-family rental houses is that there is time to work on the projects in between other obligations or services. For my landscape company, we were finding it hard to find something that wouldn't take away from our existing obligations and could be done on the side during any downtime. This option was perfect because there was not an immediate rush or deadline to turn a property into a rentable home.

By this one simple thought of keeping good employees and enhancing their skills, I was able to create year-round work for my staff and another business on the side. It was a win-win situation for everyone. Eventually this new corollary business was built into a great portfolio of properties with cash flow every month and build appreciation, all while not having to lay anyone off during the slower months.

Think deeply about what corollaries you may or may not be able to implement into your business. What assets and equipment do you have? What skills do you and your staff possess that can transfer to another venture? What are some things that you wish you could do or want to do down the road? In order to cross sell or upsell your customers, you first need to plan and figure out your future goals. Once your goals are mapped out, you can then begin to create a game plan to implement those add-on products and strategically plan what steps need to be put in place now so that you can offer that service or product down the line.

Now think about what your company is currently doing and what you may be getting from other vendors, suppliers, or support companies. Most business owners don't think about this area of expansion. By noting all of the vendors and everybody that you're currently using, you may also be able to explore and capitalize into one of those industries. Select the easiest option first. How would you be able to bring that under one company or start up a separate company just to help out your current business model?

An example of this methodology may be a car sales company that is paying for somebody to detail and wash all their cars. You can easily set up a department or designated staff to perform this work and keep all that money in-house. By creating this new division, you are not only bringing in additional revenue, but you also are growing another avenue of business that you may soon be able to offer to other car dealerships in town.

The real estate industry recently utilized this ideology as well. Most brokerages were only representing the buyers and sellers and had to use outside companies for services like inspections and title work. Many in the not so near past started other companies that brought these services all under one roof to make the process easier for both the clients and agents and also benefited by bringing in another income stream.

Consider the unlimited number of options when trying to implement corollary products, services, and even businesses. The sky is the limit, and this is where true wealth is created. Throughout my entire schooling and business college experience, I was never taught about the process of looking for additional corollaries. I was told to focus on one thing I was good at and not overextend or get greedy. Most truly successful entrepreneurs come to understand the external view of finding accompanying products or services. This concept though is what truly sets them apart from the masses and the average.

By viewing your operations and being aware of possible opportunities, you will have a better understanding of how to grow not only your business but also your entire portfolio of companies. Everyone starts with a dream with a great product or service, but once you create it, you must shift your thought process into horizontal growth dreams.

Exercises:

1. Write down your current services and products and list what corollaries for each division you think would complement the original sale.
2. What are your clients buying from your competition that you can bring in-house or start new companies to provide?
3. Make a list of all current assets, equipment, and skills your company has and how you can leverage them to create new opportunities.
4. Where are you spending money with vendors, supplies, and more that you may be able to bring in-house under one roof?

CHAPTER 5

BUILD ON THE CUSTOMER

Believe it or not, existing customers are more crucial to business growth than finding new ones. Most entrepreneurs forget this key fact and constantly seek out selling to as many new customers as possible. By focusing on your main clients first, you will be able to offer more corollary products and services to customers that already know and trust your business.

Realize that without your existing customers, your company would not exist. Don't take this for granted and create a bond with each and every client to show them how much you appreciate them; make them feel important.

The quest for horizontal growth has an imperative need for expanding on your existing clientele.

Studies have shown that by simply increasing your customer retention rates by 5 percent increases profits by 25 percent to 95 percent, according to research done by Frederick Reichheld of Bain & Company.[25]

Though this statistic is quite broad, it proves a valid point that no matter what, you must retain and keep your current clientele satisfied, period. You must constantly provide the best customer service above all else. Even if your product isn't the best out in the market, your attention to your clients supersedes all else. If you have the willingness to provide the best service and attention, there is nothing stopping you from greatness.

Your existing clients are a major asset to your company. Treat each and every one of them as though they are the most important customer to your company. Although this may be hard to accomplish at times with difficult or picky customers, you must still take this approach.

Even the most difficult clients are paying for a product or service, and you must praise them for working with you and not your competitors.

25   Fred Reichheld, "Prescription for Cutting Costs," *Bain & Company,* Acssessed October 25, 2020.

You won't believe how many times I have had to work with these difficult clients. Whether it is the customer that expects everything for free, critiques your product or service, or the ones that call and text all hours of the night and on weekends, everyone will soon experience more difficult people to work with.

Sure, it seems easy to raise your voice or argue back and forth with them, but by keeping a calm attitude and offering them the best customer service, you never know what will come out of your business relationship. In my mind, I figure if my company can work effectively with these more particular individuals, then all our other clients' needs will seem remarkably more manageable.

I've had numerous clients that most companies would never want to deal with. Once we treated these customers with the highest respect, we were astonished at how many referrals we ended up getting from them. The fact is that once these particular people find someone that will work with them and their needs, they will praise your work and your company. These customers tend to tell more people than the clients that are much more laid-back and tranquil.

This mindset has been spoken about by many successful people throughout time. A great friend of mine, Van Deeb, founder of Deeb Realty in Omaha, Nebraska, would tell me, "Every person I meet, I make them feel that they are the most important person in the room while talking to them." Van was the epitome of treating all his customers, employees, and anyone he met in public in the highest regard.

With this one focused trait, Van broke through all competition and at that time had one of the fastest growing real estate firms in the country. People wanted to do business with him and his team. They yearned to feel important and be taken care of, and as a result, he was able to grow his business into a company that employed over 350 agents.

Van's message sticks with my team and me daily. We do everything we can to make sure that clients are taken care of. You must drop everything and do whatever you need to do to please them. By doing so you continue to prove your worth and value with your products and services. This value will be far greater than anything your clients have ever experienced before, and they will continue to give you business in return.

So many companies out there will not answer their clients' calls or return voicemails or emails within a timely fashion. Imagine what the customer must feel when they call your office phone and have to wait several hours or even several days for you to get back to them. To them, it appears you don't want or don't need their business and do not appreciate them at all.

This is one of the easiest ways to provide your clients with a better service than your competition. Many times, I have actually tried to give companies business, but they never returned my calls or emails. Can you imagine that? I was willing and ready to spend money with them, and they had the audacity to not get back to me. This character and habit should never be allowed in your organization—ever. Always return calls, texts, and emails, even if you are busy. I use a simple reply stating that I have received the message and will get back to them with the information they are seeking as soon as possible.

See, that isn't that hard to do, is it? Even if you are completely swamped with work or unavailable, you can let the client know that you have at least received the message and will service them shortly.

There was a time while my companies were growing that I didn't want to give out my personal phone number to certain clients. I felt I was already engrossed with work and this would be a distraction to my day-to-day activities. I dreaded the Friday-night calls or texts after-hours.

After realizing that I was actually hindering my growth, I quickly started to give my personal number out to any client that asked—especially the very picky ones. I would rather talk to them as soon as possible and handle any situations to give them the highest value I could provide for our products and services. I wanted to make them feel that they could always talk to someone, no matter what time it was.

Sure, I would get some calls at 10:00 p.m. or later on the weekends when I was already in bed about ready for sleep. I handled this very easily, however. I would normally set an alarm earlier than normal for the gym or to go into the office, maybe around 5:00 a.m. and would call that customer back first thing. Most times they did not answer because they were sleeping, so I would leave them a message apologizing that I missed their call because I was in bed and that I called back as soon as I saw their missed call. I would also mention to them what times they can expect to reach me moving forward. By getting back to these people as soon as possible, I was able to build trust with clients and show them how important they are to my company.

Although this may not be the most orthodox way to handle things, sometimes you need to let the client know that there is a fine line with communication and that everyone has different sleep and family schedules. What might be early for them at 10:00 p.m. correlates to some people being early risers. They seem to get this point very quickly.

No matter the circumstances, it is still easier to retain these customers than find new ones. These customers will continue to buy from you and work with you far longer when you treat them with the utmost importance. You must focus on your existing customers before seeking out new ones. You have a much better position at increasing revenue through this avenue than any other.

According to the Brevet Group, retaining your current customers is six to seven times less costly than acquiring new clients.[26] This statistic is a very important one to remember. Understand that the price to find and acquire new customers is a very costly one. You must put your time and resources into keeping existing clients happy which will in turn boost your re-order business.

---

26 Brian Williams, "21 Mind-Blowing Sales Stats," *The Brevet Group,* Accessed October 26, 2020.

WHY YOU NEED TO ASK QUESTIONS

So how can you ensure your customers are happy and continue to purchase from you? How do you know if they need any additional help or have questions about current products or sales? The easiest way to find out is to ask questions and simply talk to them. Whether you are meeting in person or over the phone, there are plenty of ways to retain and grow your client base. By asking questions you will be able to offer more products and services to your clients. By acquiring more complimentary services, you will begin to build your horizontal growth.

I love meeting with customers or potential clients in person. This one-on-one aspect gives you the ability to relate on a much more personal and welcoming level with them. When meeting with clients, I always start by asking how their day is going or how their weekend was to break the ice.

For me, this type of communication comes easy. I love meeting people and just striking up conversations. For some that are more introverted, you may find this to be a difficult task, but just remember that you are viewing these clients as you would a good friend; you just don't know it yet.

This short intro is a way to ask them more about their hobbies and interests and bring the professionalism to a more personable level.

This is one easy way to build on your current clients. I always ask and remember what they enjoy doing, whether that is to go camping, work on their motorcycles, or if they like a good bottle of wine. By understanding and knowing these characteristics, you can relate on a non-business level whenever you connect with them in the future. It is also great to know and remember this information if you ever decide to gift the customer certain items. If they enjoy a cabernet wine, then I will drop off a nice bottle after closing a large deal.

I love to chat about their interests and what they are passionate about. It is truly the small things that will set you apart, and by knowing your customer, you will gain more respect and business.

You must be sincere though. Treat the client as a close acquaintance or friend and never like you are using them. This will come out as being more genuine, and people will begin to notice your true appreciation of meeting with them.

During these discussions, I also will always bring up things that I see or that I believe will enhance their lives. Typically it is something that ties back to a product or service we can offer them; regarding my landscaping company, maybe it is simply recurring maintenance of their landscape beds. I know this chore will take away a lot of the client's time from being with their family or doing a hobby, so why not simply let a professional take care of it and be able to enjoy what they love? Tying in the advantages of utilizing more of your products or services not only benefits their lives but is also how you continue to grow the revenue from existing clients.

By putting these pieces together, you will see that they are more apt to work with you when it helps alleviate stress or allows them to create more time, which for most is more valuable than money itself. Even if I don't bring it up to the client directly, I take notes of what I saw or can offer to them and reach out at a later time. I would let them know how grateful I was to meet and speak with them and that I also noticed XYZ during our visit and that we would be happy to offer any assistance they may need in the future.

You would be astonished at how many secondary sales come out of this simple process. Your client is already engaged with your company and gives you the advantage to create future partnership. By not capitalizing on or bonding with your customers, you would be greatly hindering your future growth.

UPSELLING

Treating your customers better than your competition enables you to upsell other products that would go hand in hand with your products they are currently using.

An easy example of upselling is when you are looking to buy a car. Auto manufacturers always implement the option of upselling on nicer models of cars no matter what the brand. The option of seeing vehicles that are the exact same frame and body style but have more perks as they get more expensive always seems to intrigue buyers into buying a more expensive model.

Let's say you are looking to buy a Mercedes S-Class Sedan which starts around $95,000 for the S 450. There is always an option to get something more. Whether the vehicle has more horsepower or a few more high-tech amenities, customers will quickly see the perks of stepping up. For example, you can compare to other upgrades including the AMG S 63 option that starts off at $151,000 and additional options go up from there.

So why do these companies offer so many varieties of what is essentially the same vehicle? According to studies by Limelight, a psychological decision goes through buyers' minds when they see a more expensive vehicle with more options than they were originally looking for. It may be for self-esteem, comfort, or a status symbol, and the car industry knows this very well and capitalizes on the socio-psychological decisions buyers make.[27]

If these manufacturers didn't provide these other options for upselling of cars that are essentially the same, they would be leaving billions of dollars on the table. They know and understand that buyers have these psychological thoughts that account for their self-esteem, comfort, or desire to reach a certain status. Manufacturers know it is big business.

When someone goes in to buy the S 450 and sees the S 550 sitting right next to it, they mentally start comparing and contemplating why they would settle for the lowest model. The salesperson can easily point out the differences and perks by jumping up a level in model for comparison. It's an extra $10,000, but in their mind, it makes perfect sense for all the extra add-ons and status.

And just like that, the salesperson is able to increase their commission and easily provide the customer with a higher

27   Julia Manoukian, "The Psychology of Luxury Car Buyers: 7 Considerations," *Limelight,* November 27, 2019.

end product they weren't originally going to purchase. Sure, this doesn't happen all the time, but the buyer that purchases the lowest model tends to step up on their next purchase. Without seeing those upsell options, they would not know what else is out there.

You must be able to offer multiple levels of products and services to your clients to achieve horizontal success. To start, I would recommend having a basic model or service that will fit your customers' needs and then having a premium product that you can bump them up to. This premium sale may include better materials, more frequent services, or even a VIP experience, depending on your business. By showing the customer they have options, it allows them to have the choice to determine their needs and level of service.

This one easy step of creating different levels of products will create a new income stream that will contribute to an organization. While most don't offer this type of service, you will be able to capture a larger market audience with your horizontal thinking.

Without offering different levels, you are not allowing the customer to truly choose what level of service they require. Some don't want the cheapest product or service. They would rather spend extra money to ensure they have the best of the best.

CROSS-SELLING

Travis Freeman's Brite Idea holiday-lighting company is a perfect example of the opportunity to cross-sell. When clients come into his showroom thinking they want to purchase lights for the roof of their home, they discover hundreds—if not thousands—of other products that can be added onto their current design to enhance the overall appearance of their decor. They might see greenery or even pot decor that can add accents to the design.

Without having cross-selling corollaries, you are inhibiting your sales and business. You must give options to your customers and be able to enhance their products or services or they will buy elsewhere.

It's been said that second money is easier to get than first money. Once a customer is okay with spending money with you, it is far easier for them to add on additional sales.

Think about the last time you shopped at a store to get a suit or a pair of jeans. Do you realize how easy it is to toss in a belt or a tie to the order? You are already spending several hundred or thousands of dollars, so what is another fifty dollars going to do? It is an easy way to get a little more money out of the buyer, and this happens across all industries. The buyer typically will purchase from you as long as you have options for them to see and tie in with your main products.

You are not trying to deceive your customer or pressure them into buying something that they do not want. By cross-selling to existing customers, you are offering items or services to enhance their overall satisfaction with the first order.

This tactic is by far the easiest way to increase sales compared to finding new customers. According to the book, *Marketing Metrics,* "Businesses have a 60–70% chance of creating additional sales to an existing customer, while the probability of selling to a new prospect is only 5–20%."[28] This statistic shows it is much more probable and important to service your existing customers and offer additional corollary products for them to choose from.

In the lawn and landscape industry, we have numerous options to cross-sell to our clients. Let's say we are installing a new landscape around your home. In addition to the trees, plants, and landscape beds, you may find that you would like landscape lighting to enhance your landscaping or a bubbling-boulder water feature or even more expensive rock groundcover instead of mulch. We offer endless amounts of choices when it comes to providing additional options for our clients. If we only offered one bland choice, we would be limiting the amount of creativity and overall appearance our customers are looking for. You must have options and cross-selling corollaries to succeed and not become stagnant.

With all of these options to increase your sales, you must never forget rule number one.

---

28 Patrick Hull, "Don't Get Lazy about Your Client Relationships," *Forbes,* December 6, 2013.

> Always, always, always listen and take care of your clients' needs.

You won't have the opportunity to upsell or cross-sell if you don't truly understand what your customers are thinking or wanting. Once you are able to identify what your buyers genuinely are looking for, you can then seek areas of improvement and opportunities to offer different levels of service. Then you will be able to create options to increase your buyers' experience and increase sales.

Realize that without your existing customers, your company would not exist. Don't take this for granted; create a bond with each and every client to show them how much you appreciate them. Make them feel important. The quest for horizontal growth is necessary to expand upon your existing clientele.

Exercises:

1. What does your current customer interaction look like? How can you improve this process?
2. List out all your current products and services and look at ways to create a superior version to upsell.
3. List out all your current products and services and accompanying cross-sell options that will go hand in hand with the original sales.
4. What are some ways you can make your clients feel important? What can you provide them to ensure they think they matter to you?

CHAPTER 6

SIMPLIFYING

———

"Almost all quality improvement comes via simplification of design, manufacturing, layout, processes, and procedures."[29]

- TOM PETERS

In addition to generating more sales with your existing clientele in your quest for horizontal growth, simplifying your business means your ideas will cause more opportunities to rise to the surface. In this chapter we will break down several different places to start looking for simplification when trying to obtain horizontal growth. From the moment you start your day to the moment you lay down for bed, there are opportunities to simplify your schedule to optimize and capitalize upon your growth potential.

Everyone goes through a time when they begin to grow and actually overthink numerous ideas for their business. In the end, those thoughts require complex formulations and integrations to launch those ideas. People spend hours on end

———

29   "Tom Peters Quotes," *All Great Quotes,* Accessed October 15, 2020.

coming up with the next best thing or a unique advantage to the market, when all along, gold mine ideas are simply right under their noses. Things can easily be added to your company to gain horizontal success without coming up with the next big idea or a world-changing piece of technology.

I truly connected to a recent article in *Entrepreneurship* magazine that linked this ideology. "Simplicity can take you a long way. The key to keeping entrepreneurship simple is to not get caught up in your own head and thoughts. Don't be overconfident with your plans or be apprehensive about your decisions. Keep your thoughts in the present while you work toward your futuristic goals. The pivotal aspect of being simple is being mindful of everything you do."[30]

Many entrepreneurs I have known have dreamed big yet failed or remained stagnant. Why is this? Many reasons helped contribute to this failure, but I truly believe the main reason is that they made things too difficult. They tried to conquer the world with ideas and theories that never came to fruition. In my opinion, they were not able to simplify their business. Though by failing and realizing where there were issues, many of these entrepreneurs tend to come back bigger than ever.

Don't get me wrong, I am a huge dreamer and see myself with limitless potential in my lifetime. Though this is what most people think entrepreneurship is, there is a way to weed

---

30 Sarvesh Shashi, "How Not to Complicate—Keeping Entrepreneurship Simple," *Entrepreneurship India,* September 3, 2018.

through these thoughts to build the base blocks to your overall goals.

When you complicate your dreams and businesses, you are destined to fail.

Figure out a way to simplify and create streamlines throughout every aspect of your business, or you will never establish proper horizontal achievements. You are your own worst enemy by spreading your goals too wide and too thin. Many people never want to accept change and are so headstrong that, unfortunately, they won't change their current processes.

These same people want to continue with the way business had been done in the past that was working for them. They don't know that one small change may make a difference of millions or even billions of dollars. There is a reason the successful people of the world create ways to simplify their industries, and by doing so, they are able to capitalize on sales and growth.

At one point in my life, I was obsessed with dreaming so big and thinking of outrageous ideas that I pictured would be industry disrupters. While this is a characteristic of most successful people, it is also a deterrent to some degree. Some ideas and thoughts honestly were a bit out of my reach. Others were so outlandish at the time that they would have required insane amounts of capital and resources.

I'm sure you've been there as well. You wanted to create something so unique and to have the ideology to change the world, but at the time, there wasn't any way of financially achieving or even starting to create a roadmap to those ideas. Though these ideas and thoughts make us who we are, they pull us away from the "easy money," as I like to call it. These simplified opportunities can grow into business decisions which in turn create revenue right now. Inevitably these simple changes create a foundation to build upon in the future to hopefully achieve those lifelong goals.

Brainstorming ideas, while productive, is a time when you can easily go on tangents which pull you further from your quest of building properly. In this chapter, I will illustrate the proper way to plan and implement new ideas by focusing on corollary opportunities. You will be amazed at how quickly you can reach success by doing so.

KISS: This terminology has been around for a long time. KISS: "keep it simple silly" still plays a major part in business no matter at what level you are currently. The more you reduce complication and focus on simplifying all aspects of your business, the more successful you will become.

At any given moment of your daily routine, something can always be optimized. However, it's damn near impossible to have all your processes and business routines simplified 100 percent. Something will come along that will improve your business over time and make life easier. Whether it is technology or just consummating a new routine improvement, there is always room to improve.

The key is to keep an open mind. Once you are set in your ways, it is more difficult to break the chains of change. You must continue to seek out new ideas to optimize and simplify your organization in all aspects to create a more streamlined and profitable company.

HOW SIMPLIFICATION WORKED FOR ONE ENTREPRE-NEUR

A very successful tech entrepreneur and friend, Guinio Volpone, discussed this ideology of simplification with me when we recently met. We talked about the keys to simplifying business to reach heightened success and how important it truly is. Guinio told me, "Whether it is a tech company or a brick-and-mortar business, there is always a way to outsource or simplify your day-to-day processes."

Guinio started looking to simplify existing processes in his twenties when he began in the ticketing industry. His innovation and ability to find ways to simplify the ticketing industry are what have helped him go from scalping tickets in college to working with some of the biggest sports organizations and boards in the US and eventually building Seat Scouts, a company among several others managing billions of dollars in inventory.

Guinio's Seat Scouts business is an automation tool he found that was needed in his first business to help solve a problem. He went on to say, "I was building this software to simplify my company, and then we were able to see the voids in the industry and leased it out for other brokers." This platform created the ability to offer everything from fulfillment, distribution, accounting, and a gamut of other perks to help out others in his industry. "I was just looking at what was out there but didn't find anything that met our needs, and we decided it was time to create a corollary company that would not just benefit us but the entire industry."

By creating a platform which helped correct some of the inefficiencies in his company, he was able to catapult it to a whole new level of success. Guinio focused his attention where the issues were and in turn was able to create software that would eventually lead him to take his business to a level no one had seen before. From scalping tickets to working with major professional sports leagues and organizations, he truly found a way to simplify the processes in his company and his industry.

This thought process and ability to seek out simplification is what separates those that want success from those that are simply content. I'm sure everyone in your industry wants something better that will help simplify their businesses, but how many actually take the leap to develop an easier process? It is something that the go-getters find and capitalize on.

UTILIZE YOUR STAFF

Each winter my management team discusses ways to optimize all aspects of our company from the previous season. We break down the workflow routine and our technology needs. After laying everything out, we look at each individual process or line item and discuss if there is a way to simplify that specified duty. You would be amazed at how many great ideas will come out of involving your staff in these sessions.

These ideas may be areas of your company that you would never have thought to look. While you have an overhead view of your company, your staff sees each individual task being performed day in and day out across the organization.

Your staff are the ones who deal with these duties on a daily basis, and no one else has a better sense of how to incorporate simplicity in your company than your team. I have stopped keeping track of the many ideas my staff has suggested that we have implemented. Whether it's an overall organizational simplification or implementing a new widget for a specific task, everyone on your team wants to improve their daily duties. It creates a better work environment, saves money, and also creates ease for their job tasks. Without the help of your employees, you will never gain new insights into your industry or ideas that will give you a competitive advantage that will eventually allow you to focus on adding corollary options to build horizontally.

So let's keep it simple. Let's find out all the processes of your day-to-day business process and break down each step of the day. By doing so, you can look at each indicator and brainstorm whether there is an improvement in that area or not. If there isn't, great! You have simplified that process to perfection. However, you never know, as time goes on, you may revisit this process and find a new implementation that will benefit your company.

For the other areas of your business, you will be shocked by the many things you can do to simplify your processes or implement new growth opportunities. Two routes present themselves.

The first is to discover where any areas of wasted time or resources are hiding. This can be any outdated or overcomplicated processes. Examples of this could be writing paper invoices or not utilizing technology in your operations. You may also find wasted, unutilized materials or equipment that isn't being used that you could incorporate into new products or services for your clients. You will find many ways to simplify these inefficiencies within your business. By pulling together your staff, you can hear different opinions on how to solve and overcome these issues to create a cohesive and profitable workflow.

The second ideology that can be implemented is by brainstorming new growth opportunities throughout the entire company. What areas can you cut out a step of your day-to-day processes by implementing a new idea or a piece of technology? Is there a piece of equipment that will increase your production time or lower downtime? What is out there that can give you an advantage over the competition to create more revenue? And potentially, what new service can be offered to help solve a problem that you may face?

I'm a big believer in doing what you do best and letting someone else do the things that take away your energy to create more sales, whether that be cleaning your offices or something as simple as having to make coffee each morning and throughout the day. We have found people and vendors to take over these rolls for a minimal cost, which allows us to focus on bigger and better things.

These are all very important points that you should be investigating with your team. These key methods to find inefficiencies to simplify are the pillars to gain horizontal growth without racking your brain to come up with the next biggest and brightest idea.

If you simplify to create corollary opportunities in all areas of your business, inevitably, you will attain proper growth. By finding ways to simplify, not only are you able to free up more cash to grow into corollary ideas, but you can also utilize your existing business staff, assets, building, and supplies to grow horizontally. Let's take a look at a few more things that have significantly helped me during the growth of my companies.

During management meetings, we uncovered ways to simplify. First, we realized we were starting to get maxed out on our workload. We did so by writing down each of our responsibilities on a whiteboard. Because each of us was overloaded, we weren't able to bring in more revenue. So, we decided to hire more help for those overloaded duties.

Recently, for one of my companies, we found that marketing was taking time away from more than one person and hired a marketing strategist. You may not realize this, but hiring a person like a marketing strategist not only helps simplify your company advertising, but it is also a corollary in itself. Since the hiring of this individual, we have been able to tremendously increase our online social media presence and bring in new customers quicker than ever before. It has gotten to the point where this team member is having to help answer phone calls because we are getting too many leads and inquiries!

If we hadn't thought about simplifying our day-to-day activities and passing them onto someone else, we would not have been able to continue growing at the rate we currently are. We have created impeccable brand awareness and reached clients that would not have normally chosen our company over the competition.

"Growth creates complexity, which requires simplicity."[31]

- ANDY STANLEY

A key point to keep in mind comes from a report from Heidrick & Struggles research in which they state: "Organizations are in a state of simplicity when activity is aligned with strategy. These organizations must create a culture where simplicity prevails by fostering a new way of behavior." The report goes on to state that simplicity is achieved by "decluttering" your organization through regular and repeatable interventions.[32]

When reaching this point in business, growth seems to be stressful and exciting at the same time. It's a point all successful entrepreneurs reach in their journey. This stressfulness of growth, however, is a great thing—don't ever forget that. Although it may seem complex or cause mental strain, you must realize that it is a necessary hurdle on the way to success. We have all experienced this—me included!

---

31 Josh Daffern, "Seven Great Quotes from the Chick-Fil-a Leadercast," *Patheos,* May 13, 2013.

32 Alice Breeden and Adam Howe, "Why Simplicity Is the Key to Accelerating Performance," *Heidrick & Struggles,* December 5, 2019.

You have to take a step back and realize that billions of people would give anything to be in your shoes. They would give everything to be able to even have the opportunity you are experiencing. It is a privilege, and you should feel honored and lucky that these exciting changes are happening to you.

When times get complex and stressful, however, these are the moments you realize that simplicity is the key to pushing forward. These convoluted times of growth are actually what sets us as entrepreneurs apart from the masses. We find a way to take the labyrinth of data and struggles of growing and find alternative avenues to cut through the brush and simplify our quest to the finish line.

Just as Guinio and many others have done in their industries, you must take a step back, analyze, and simplify your processes. Only then can you capitalize upon and increase your productivity and performance. Simplifying is a large step on the path to horizontal growth. When you are able to simplify, you are able to multiply. When you multiply, you achieve true success.

Exercises:

1. Lay out your processes and identify what you can implement to simplify.
2. Is there a piece of technology you can utilize or create to simplify your business?
3. If so, would you be able to offer this technology or process to others in your industry?

4. List out your staff and your day-to-day responsibilities and seek out avenues to combine tasks, hire, or streamline any processes.

CHAPTER 7

HIRING TALENT

The late Steve Jobs of Apple summed up the importance of talent with this advice: "Go after the cream of the cream. A small team of A+ players can run circles round a giant team of B and C players."[33]

Talent on paper doesn't matter when hiring for your team. Seriously, you don't need to hire the most talented person who applies for the job! You need to seek out great people with amazing qualities and attitudes, and once you find them, you will find out how quickly your company will grow. In this chapter, we will go through the points you need to start looking for when hiring talent and what it takes to build a proper employee community.

WHY HIRING THE RIGHT PEOPLE IS IMPORTANT

When I was recently speaking with Ron Carson about how he was able to amass so much horizontal and positive growth

---

33 Scott Keller and Mary Meaney, "Attracting and Retaining the Right Talent," *McKinsey & Company*, November 24, 2017.

within his companies, he always circled back to one main point: hiring great people.

Ron stated, "If someone has a great attitude, I can teach them anything, and if they have a terrible attitude, I can't teach them anything."

He didn't care how talented the individual was, as long as he or she fit his company culture. He went on to say, "Don't just hire people like yourself, hire people that are going to challenge you and have a different thinking, someone that brings a real care, a love, and a thought to your business. They should also share a common vision and mission for the future."

Ron's words are a true testament of hiring the right people and talent that will in turn propel you and your company to its goals. Seeking out a great attitude and a willingness to learn far exceeds anyone with a perfect resume or college degree. These individuals may seem to be perfect fits but may be a difficult person with whom to work.

Studies have shown that approximately 82 percent of Fortune 500 executives don't believe that their companies recruit highly talented people. In the same study, of these executives, only 14 percent actually knew who the high and low performers of their companies were.[34]

Believe me, I have gone this route many times in the past and soon came to find out that someone who does not fit the

_____

34 Ibid.

culture or professionalism does not last very long. You have to remember that these team members are actually going to be part of your family. You will most likely see them for more hours of the day than your biological family! You need to make sure they are people that bring great morale and character to your company because, in the end, they represent you and your company, and your company image is something that you never want to have tarnished.

At times, I used to hastily look for new talent to join my team because we were very desperate for staffing help and needed to bring people on board as soon as possible. Even if their attitude was not great but they had skills, we would still hire them because we needed the support so badly to provide the work to our customers. This was a terrible idea to follow for the business.

Not too far down the road, we soon realized that these individuals did not have the drive or passion for their jobs. They actually ended up costing the company money because we had to fix the mistakes they created. In some cases, they simply didn't do the work they were hired to do. Not only did it cost us monetarily, it also discouraged existing employees by not bringing on the proper talent to begin with.

It's been said by many people that a bad attitude is like a cancer. If not taken care of right away, that negativity will spread throughout your organization and become toxic. It must be addressed or removed to provide a more conducive work environment and positive outlook for expansion.

Without having these experiences, I would have never learned that this theory was actually true. Attitude is everything. It can't be taught, but skills can be learned. I would much rather hire someone based on their attitude and teach those individuals the skills than the other way around.

A great attitude is contagious and will truly lift up your team through thick and thin. Focusing on talented individuals with great attitudes will help you achieve any milestone and overcome any hurdles.

Without attracting and adding the right talent to your company's work force, you are going to inhibit your growth to achieve diversified success. This is a crucial part in building a prosperous company. You must get the right people in place before you look to grow horizontally. If not, you may have to backtrack and fix issues that were not properly instilled, which will slow your progress and limit your capabilities.

We all know that great owners can't build a successful business alone. Having a great team working with you elevates your business success. To create a well-oiled, thriving, and successful organization, you will need to understand how to attract, retain, and reward your team members. This vital aspect of a business has many different avenues to appeal to these individuals, and I will walk you through the most important process of building your team.

Whether you are the only person in your company or have five hundred employees, there is still a proper way to attain talented individuals. Although this idea may seem daunting and scary for newly established entrepreneurs, there is a proper time when you should factor in your need to hire the right talent to help your organization grow.

You cannot build an empire by yourself. You must find great team members that want to join you along the way. There was never a Roman ship that was led to victory by one man. It took a brotherhood of men to row that vessel to a greater cause.

HIRING FOR GROWTH AND DIVERSIFICATION

So when is the right time to search for talent? When should you seek out help to join you on the quest for success?

As stated in the previous chapter, I believe that you should always hire when looking to simplify. When you have reached a point that you are capped out on your daily regiments and potential, you should start seeking out new team members.

According to Jennifer Maffei of VEA Services, "The average entrepreneur wastes at minimum two hours per day on emails, phone calls, scheduling, re-scheduling, and research. Multiply those two hours by five days, and you're losing 10 hours a week, and over the course of a year, accumulates to approximately three months of work time or 520 hours".[35]

---

35 Wendy Keller, "The 3-Step Process to Hiring Your First Assistant," *The Hour,* November 29, 2018.

Now, if you are managing more than one business, you can multiply those hours by two, three, or even more. Your day gets filled with the most basic tasks, and soon you are stressed and unable to focus on building your businesses. Mind you, these are the most basic tasks and not even the duties to provide service to your customers.

If you are like me, I spend well over two hours per day at minimum on the above tasks. Just today, on my phone, I have made or taken thirty four calls and sent over fifty text messages. You don't realize it, but this is taking valuable time away from more important roles and building your business. Granted, some of these texts and calls were in fact to create revenue and sales. Although this is just on my personal cell phone, many other things such as emails, scheduling, and office work build on top of this in my daily routine.

You can improve your productivity and growth by hiring talent and delegating duties. Though you may never be able to fully take all your duties off your plate, you have the ability to appoint different tasks by theoretically cloning yourself.

To get into the mindset and ability to hire new talent, you need to imagine if you could in fact clone yourself and your attitude to increase productivity, drive, and work ethic. How amazing would that be? How much more work would you be able to accomplish on a day-to-day basis? How many more sales could you make, and how much larger could your company get? The idea of multiplying yourself needs to be in the back of your mind around every aspect of your organization in order to attain true horizontal growth.

This step is the most important to anyone looking to expand their business, period. It has helped me tremendously with the success of my company. Before you even begin to hire, you must do this task: Think about everything you do within a typical workday, inside and outside of work. Where do you spend your time? Take note of all the tasks that have taken your time away from building your business and success. For most industries, your entrepreneurial schedule may look like the following: billing, payroll, marketing, cleaning, sales meetings, data entry, bookkeeping, and more.

These are all very important duties that must be done while building your business. In the beginning stages of most companies, entrepreneurs will do all of these tasks until cash flow begins to come in. It's normal and is exactly what I was doing as well. I was the bookkeeper, the human resource personnel, the producer, the marketing team, the janitor, and the customer service team all within one position.

During the rapid growth of my company, I remember having to do production services during the day. Then, from 5:00 p.m. on, I would work in the office billing out clients, managing the financials, and other back office work. It wasn't abnormal to work more than one hundred hours a week. I do not regret any of it, as it shaped me to be who I am today with my companies. However, I was burning the candle at both ends, and I was about to run out of wax.

It was after some time that my close friend Travis Freeman taught me something that I will never forget. He gave me a tip that I continue to incorporate throughout my organizations. He told me that by writing down the daily duties I was doing and seeing where I spent my time, I would see where I needed to look to hire talent. I needed to focus on hiring someone to take over the tasks where I was working within my business rather than working *on* my business.

You must truly think of how you can pass along the work that consumes most of your daily schedule to another individual to remove it from your plate. Otherwise, you will never gain horizontal growth. This must happen, no matter if you are just starting out in business or are the CEO of a $100 million company.

Travis went on to explain that if I was spending 50 percent of the workday billing out invoices and doing office paperwork, then I should be able to hire someone to take over those tasks. With the extra time that would be opened up by creating a new position, I would be able to focus on actually building the business by making phone calls, meeting potential customers, and reaching out to existing clients to increase sales, all of which should end up covering the salary of the person that I just hired.

Before hearing this information, I was scared to make the leap and pay a salaried employee to come on board full-time only for office work. I didn't think I could afford to hire someone to take on these duties, and I was worried that I wasn't ready yet. After hearing this advice, it made perfect sense, and I was able to make a leap of faith knowing that I would easily be able to create enough sales to cover that position.

Not only would this person take on the duties I was once performing, but they would have additional time to pick up other tasks and help with specialty assignments to fill in when needed.

If you do this with your business, this team member will bring in new ideas and provide a different perspective. When you bring someone in that learns your processes from scratch, you learn different ways and more efficient processes that will improve your company. This will also help establish a strong mindset to think outside the box. Remember that you are hiring for personality and attitude and that these traits will take you much further in horizontal growth potential than anything else.

With this growth opportunity in front of you and time to build your company, do you think that you can create at least a new position and focus on increasing your overall sales? Of course you can! You can finally focus on working on your business. You will soon find that you can quickly move to working on more critical tasks and growth planning opportunities. I guarantee that you will pay for that newly appointed team member's salary in no time!

By adopting this practice from Travis, I was able to implement it across all areas of my business. With the free time I had opened up I would look for corollaries in my industry and focus on selling them. Soon, there would be enough interest and sales coming in that the new product or service would begin to take up more of my daily time. At this point, I knew I needed to multiply myself again and hire someone to take on that new responsibility and manage that other area of the company.

You can see how easy it is to quickly create and grow corollary products and services when you have the proper time to focus on the research to build them. Using this hiring model will take your business and entire organization to the next level.

Now that you understand the process of expanding your team, you can utilize this approach and multiply yourself as your company grows. You will find that as you grow, the people you hired will soon need to perform this exact same exercise to create more positions based on the growth of their duties. As one department continues to grow, you will need to add more people to tackle the day-to-day tasks to run and expand your business.

This process has been one of the greatest attributes to the growth of my companies. It has provided the opportunity to achieve horizontal growth by adding talented individuals and has created a smoother workflow where everyone knows their assigned duties. Before you can reach true success, you much focus on continuous expansion and hiring talent along the way.

Exercises:

1. Write down all the tasks you do that make up your daily routine.
2. Which duties or combination of duties can you delegate or hire someone to manage?
3. Make a list of proactive activities you would be able to accomplish with additional time in your day.

CHAPTER 8

MASTERING ANALYTICAL THINKING

———

Here's the deal. Plenty of successful entrepreneurs crush it in business but will eventually plateau or start declining over time. I get it, it happens and is part of the economic cycle of trends and businesses. But it does not have to be this way. There are ways to analyze and foresee future trends before your products and services are ever impacted. By looking deep into your processes and financials, you will be able to overcome any loss of income, cut divisions that don't make money, and focus on profitable avenues to reach your goals of horizontal growth and success.

Andrew Chen, former head of rider growth at Uber stated, "It's important to leverage data the same way, whether it's a strategic or tactical issue: Have a vision for what you are trying to do. Use data to validate and help you navigate that vision and map it down into small enough pieces where you can begin to execute in a data-informed way. Don't let shallow analysis of data that happens to be cheap or easy or fast to collect nudge you off course in your entrepreneurial pursuits."[36]

When Chen started working at Uber in 2015, their revenue was approximately $2 billion.[37] With Chen's help to analyze the data and implement a tactical strategy, they were able to reach a revenue of $49.8 billion when Chen left in 2018.[38]

Every entrepreneur will find their own way to analyze and go through the areas that need improvement in their businesses. Each owner and each industry may have a favorable method that makes sense for your organization. For my own businesses, I truly believe that being able to make analytical decisions all goes back to your profit and loss statement (P&L).

THE ESSENTIAL P&L STATEMENT

The P&L statement, also known as the income statement, shows all your income, costs of goods (typically materials that are needed to create a product), and expenses, which allows you to calculate your net income.

When starting out in business, follow the traditional P&L statement with your most common income sources, your main cost of goods sold (COGS), and your expenses to get

---

36   Andrew Chen, "Know the Difference between Data-Informed and versus Data-Driven," @andrewchen Newsletter, Accessed October 7, 2020.

37   Shu Zhange and Gerry Shih, "Uber Seen Reaching $10.8 Billion in Bookings in 2015: Fundraising Presentation," *Reuters,* August 21, 2015.

38   Mansoor Iqbal, "Uber Revenue and Usage Statistics (2020)," *Business of Apps,* October 30, 2020.

your net income. Almost all of your income, COGS, and expenses are bulked into a few major line items. This is a great overall view of how your business is performing and what your net income is; however, it does not give valid details of each category or explain where you are actually making or losing money.

Remember, my goal is to make you different than your competition and the masses. In doing so, I want you to think differently, which will propel you and your business to make proper decisions for success.

Although basic reporting is a great benchmark in a newly started business, you must start looking deeper into these analytics to be able to achieve horizontal expansion and eliminate those indicators that are deterring your growth. For example, we discussed the corollaries with Starbucks between coffee and add-on products that it offers for sale to its clients. If Starbucks was not able to actively review their analytical financial reports, how would the company know if certain products were actually selling at a profit in its stores?

Analytics is one of the most important components of business. It allows you to see what is working, what isn't working, and overall, what you need to plan for the future.

I have created one of the most detailed P&L statements that most people have ever seen, which includes over eleven pages of data. I made it a priority to be as detailed as possible. I wanted to be more detailed than all other companies in my industry or any other industry out there. I wanted to have an advantage over others and do things that I know most wouldn't do. By doing so, I can clearly view all of our corollary products and opportunities to double down on.

So what would the benefits of having such a detailed P&L statement be? Here's the scoop. With my lawn and landscaping company, we currently have over seven divisions, each providing countless products and numerous services under each division. When we create a new product or service, we make a new income category in our bookkeeping software, QuickBooks, to be able to track all sales, COGS, and expenses that relate to that product or service.

This is one main analytical tip I recommend you adopt. Every single product or service you offer needs to be recorded and placed on your P&L. You have to be able to track how well that income category does over the course of a year and see if it is performing well or losing money! Without proper tracking, there is no way to know if your company is profitable or not.

So here we go. You first have to identify all your products and services as an income line item. Once you have set up all your income sources, you can now implement any COGS that directly relate to each income class. You want to make sure this is as close to actual as it can be to provide you with be most accurate net income.

Now that your income and cost of goods sold are set up, it's time to set up your expenses that relate to each income-producing product or service. Whether these products or services are specific maintenance, labor, or overhead expenses such as utilities and rent, these expenses will help you figure out how profitable you will be.

A detailed P&L is especially important for horizontal growth to keep your various entrepreneurial projects organized. My lawn and landscaping business has numerous divisions in our P&L. Some of these include lawn mowing, fertilizing, irrigation, landscaping, holiday lighting, and snow removal. By seeing all the products and services we sell year to year, we are able to analyze what works and what doesn't.

To expand further, our fertilizing division has over twenty other add-on services that our technicians offer to clients. Before implementing our extremely detailed P&L philosophy we had all these services organized under one umbrella as "Fertilizing." It was so vague and broad that we weren't able to see what was even going on under this division.

On the following diagram you will see an example of our P&L statement, which only shows a few of our fertilizing-division service incomes.

Fertilizing Division Income	
6- Step Fertilizing Program	
	Step 1
	Step 2
	Step 3
	Step 4
	Step 5
	Step 6
Aeration:	
	Spring Aeration
	Fall Aeration
Overseeding:	
	Spring Overseed
	Fall Overseed
Specialty Applications:	
	Bio-solids
	Humic Acid
	Sulfer
	Gypsum
	Iron
Tree Services:	
	Pest Spraying
	Injections
	Rust Treatments
Etc:	
	Total Fertilizing Division Income

Fertilizing P&L Example

Above is simply a fraction of the breakdown of our income services under this one category. The reasoning behind a lengthy and detailed P&L statement is that you want a complete overview of what your organization is doing across all fronts. How would you know that you are losing money in a certain division or service unless you had a detailed financial statement to review? This will help to identify what works and what doesn't work and where there is opportunity for add-on corollaries to expand.

This process allows you to double or quadruple down on the income avenues that are doing well. It will even show you what items for which you may need to increase prices or even eliminate and not offer any more. You cannot be partial to certain income streams that you prefer or what your company was once built upon. You must look at this analytical data as an investment. If something isn't working, you must get rid of it or make immediate adjustments so that you are making more revenue.

Additionally, you can inspect why a certain division isn't doing well and try to correct. Remember, you already have all the numbers on each division. Maybe it is because your COGS or your expenses are too high; you are now able to think creatively about ways to reduce costs in these two aspects to turn it around and become profitable. Otherwise, I recommend scrapping the low-performing income sources and focusing on the things that are actually producing revenue and making you money.

My company was able to pinpoint the areas that were not performing as well, and then we were able to brainstorm options to turn them around. Whether it was increasing prices, additional marketing in that area, or finding a different supplier to get material prices lower, we were able to turn those segments around from low performers to become higher revenue services. Without the data to analyze, we would have continued to either lose money or break even.

My experiences prove true compared with other successful businesspeople as well. According to Carly Fiorini, former CEO of HP, "The goal is to turn data into information, and information into insight."[39] The data is there to be used to find a way to change what you are doing to become more successful.

With horizontal growth comes the responsibility to ensure you are growing properly and not just adding more to your plate that does not produce sufficient income. Focusing on analytical data helps you gain clear insight of your company so you are able to make proper decisions now instead of being blindsided with issues down the road.

SHARING DATA WITH YOUR TEAM

Once completed, this data can be discussed with your team. At a minimum, you should gather your management quarterly to discuss and go through all areas of your analytics. This is a great way to illustrate how the company is performing and show praise and appreciation for the divisions that are doing well. This also allows your team members to analyze and offer any insights or ideas on what may be improved or added to your business.

---

39 Viola Lloyd, "Turning Data Into Insight," *HRD The HR Director,* August 8, 2016.

It's amazing how many new ideas come up during these meetings by including others in your analysis of company data. Your mind has been wrapped up in this information day in and day out, and deep down, you think you know everything there is to know about your company. However, the power of sharing data is that it brings out other perspectives and thought processes that you would not normally think about. It enthusiastically boosts your management's involvement in the company, and they will embrace your organization much more than if they were left in the dark not knowing the data or the numbers.

We are very open within my company, and everyone has the opportunity to see where we stand on our numbers and growth. In one P&L meeting, I remember seeing the faces of some of our newer division members when they actually saw how much it costs to run the company. From fuel and maintenance to taxes and insurance, they were astounded at the expense amounts. They were able to realize how important it is to be efficient and continue looking for ways to cut costs or create a larger profit margin.

Sharing all the numbers has allowed me to not be the only person looking for improvements and opportunities anymore. I now have a team of people that are all looking to increase profits throughout the company by analyzing data. They know that if the company as a whole performs better and is more profitable, they will continue to get pay increases and bonuses.

At first, I was afraid and scared to show the financial data. I think this was because of how we were brought up in school and society where the boss reviews the data, and it is his or her responsibility to analyze and make improvements without help. Traditionally, many business owners have kept this information a secret and did not want to share with the employees. What a horrible idea I found that to be. The moment we opened up our books was the moment we had more individuals being happy to contribute and feeling more like a part of our company family.

No matter which route you take, periodically go through your company's analytical data. This is the backbone of your enterprise, and without being able to dissect it and dive deeply into the numbers, you will have no idea what is actually happening. You won't know where you are making money and where you are losing money.

The overall goal for your data is to see where opportunities present themselves and give you the chance to add more corollary products and services. This allows you to build on top of what you currently have working and make sure you are creating proper horizontal growth.

Exercises:

1. Break down all your income sources in as detailed a manner as possible. If you sell the same product but in different sizes, write all those down—You need to see your performers.
2. Write down any and all correlating COGS and expenses.
3. Look for any areas that cost too much or cost you money.

4. Now see what opportunities you have to expand or break down current products or services into new opportunities for sales.

3

HOW TO BUILD THE EXPANSION MINDSET

CHAPTER 9

NEW AND ASPIRING OWNERS

———

"Choose something that you both love and are good at doing."[40]
- MARK CUBAN.

Entrepreneur-billionaire Mark Cuban's quote speaks to all new and aspiring entrepreneurs. You have to believe in yourself and truly love what you do otherwise you will inevitably fail. Cuban goes on to say, "Taking that first step is always the hardest. It's terrifying, but really, it's about preparation. We all go through this process where you've got the business idea, you get that feeling in your stomach and you get all excited."[41]

---

40   Chandler Bolt, "4 Pearls of Wisdom from Inspirational Entrepreneurs," *Influencive*, November 20th, 2019.

41   Anatole Kabov, "What the Best in the Business Have to Say about Succeeding," LinkedIn, August 14, 2017.

Starting this journey is an exciting and scary one. You are going on an adventure to do something that most will never attempt or ever even want to endeavor. You are wired differently than most, and that is why you are reading this book. You want more in life, and you want to grow your empire.

Whether you are a new or aspiring entrepreneur, you have special values and beliefs that you hold dear to your personal identity. Only you can determine these values, which made you who you are and helped in your pursuit to create something from scratch, something so massive that will in turn change your and your family's financial future.

Your values and beliefs are your moral backbone. Never forget about what your entrepreneurial DNA makeup has built deep down inside of you.

In a survey conducted by Northeastern University's School of Technological Entrepreneurship, research found that nearly two-thirds of entrepreneurs claim they were inspired to start their own companies by their innate desire and determination, rather than by their education or work experience.[42]

The survey went on to find that only 1 percent of more than two hundred entrepreneurs cited higher education as a significant motivator toward starting their own venture, while

42 Leslie Taylor, "Are Entrepreneurs Born or Made?" *Inc*, October 24, 2006.

61 percent cited "innate drive." The remainder cited work experience (21 percent) and success of entrepreneurial peers within their industry (16 percent).[43]

So what do these surveys mean for you? To me, they represent what I went through growing up. I wasn't taught to become an entrepreneur. I had the drive in me the entire time. I always wanted to stay busy, create, and build. Though some do end up learning these traits throughout life and decide to start businesses as they mature, many have the DNA components to succeed from birth.

When first starting out in business and before even beginning to think about horizontal opportunities, many have a sense of self-achievement. I am certain you have the need to create something new and exciting that will benefit your customers; perhaps it's a higher quality product or service that can be taken to your market to help solve a problem. We all know this is what most aspiring entrepreneurs want to feel: the ability to create and build something from the ground up, the sense of achievement knowing that you have taken a business idea and turned it into something that actually creates income for you and others.

Self-achievement is your foundation. Once you have this feeling inside of you, you are able to plan out and attain your goals and dreams. In this book, we are not going to discuss the ins and outs of goal setting, as there are hundreds of books based on this one process. However, your goals should

---

43   Ibid.

include options to maximize horizontal growth through your existing business and starting other businesses.

YOUR REASON TO SUCCEED

For me, an overall goal is to create as many jobs throughout all my companies as I can. I want to help others create financial success working with me, not for me. I don't even care about my own salary; I don't think about it during my day-to-day routine. I am always considering how I can help my employees make more money. How can I help them better their lives and reach their goals? Once I started doing this, I could instantly see my businesses flourish. By focusing on my employees and finding ways to create higher wages, I know that my overall personal income and wealth will also increase.

You have to plan your goals out to reach maximum horizontal growth and diversification. If your goal is to help people, you need to draw out how your business is going to reach and contribute to a vast amount of individuals. What goals do you want to achieve with your new business? What dreams do you see your business achieving? How can you positively impact your community, state, or even the world? These questions have to be in the back of your mind when first starting out in business. They will help you to build, and they will provide you with a planned path to success.

Many new entrepreneurs hold the belief that they must prove success to something or someone. They need to prove to their parents or old boss that they can do something amazing. I find this common in most successful people that I have met. They want to show that they have actually made it to self-achievement based on something in their past or someone in the present.

I wasn't a perfect kid growing up, and I even got in trouble with drugs and alcohol. Although the drug I got in trouble with is now legal in most states, it was a still a burden on my parents and my reputation. I remember some of my once-called friends used to make fun of me for those bad decisions in my past as well. They didn't truly believe in me. They didn't know what I was capable of, so they took the easy way out and chose to view me as a lesser person. I even remember taking the fall in high school and being suspended to ensure others weren't punished with the same consequences. I am proud that my parents raised me to learn from my mistakes and that they continue to encourage me to do great things.

All of these things built up inside me since at a young age when I simply had the desire to prove to those haters and some school officials that looked down on me that I had succeeded. I wanted to grow as much as possible to redeem my faults in my past and to prove that I had changed and had done something amazing. In the back of my mind, I wanted to build massive businesses in order to go back to those naysayers and people that criticized me to prove to them that I had conquered my low times. I wanted to build such big businesses that I could give back more than any of them would ever think possible. I even wanted the ability to offer those naysayers jobs in one of my companies in the future.

Push out and close off any negativity and soar so far ahead that the haters can't even reach you. The great Frank Sinatra has a quote that always resonates in my mind. He stated, "The best revenge is massive success."[44]

I used those setbacks and the ridicule as a propellant for success, constantly filling my motivational engine with fuel to increase motivation. During those times, I did in fact care what those people thought of me, but deep down I knew I was meant for greatness in the end.

I truly believe the words of Sinatra. Instead of trying to get back at any naysayers or belittle them, the only thing you can do is focus on becoming such a huge success that they don't have any other option except to admire you.

Arianna Huffington, co-founder of the *Huffington Post* also went through many naysayers that tried to distract her vision and mission in business. There were critics and naysayers that tried to pull her down. Huffington states that, "When you really believe in your product, you are willing to deal with all the naysayers and persevere."[45]

These people help to fuel your drive and your dreams. Without them, life would be too easy, and you wouldn't have any motivation to create greatness. You need these people to give you the necessary push to create, to build, and to want more out of life.

---

44 Jessica Wei, *Due*, January 3, 2016.

45 Ryan Robinson, "60 Entrepreneurs Share Their Best Business Advice," *Just Luminate*, Acssessed October 29, 2020.

So take this energy and start to build your business. Plan out your venture with all your strengths and your abilities to build your company.

START BUILDING

When beginning to build a business, you may not know where to start with horizontal corollaries. The idea of expanding before you are even creating substantial revenue is scary, and I would agree 100 percent! I highly discourage taking your mind away from your initial product or service in the beginning. Stay focused, stay methodical, and remember that hard work reaps rewards.

Remember this cycle; it has gotten me where I am today, it is easy to remember, and it is a motivator every day in business:

Work hard—fail—learn a lesson—work harder

Typically, there is a proper time to start brainstorming and formulating ideas to add to your existing business model. I recommend that when you are able to sustain your current services with a proper team in place, only then can you start looking at add-on, corollary options. Your main production or service needs to run smoothly without any holes or flaws. If you can, you should try and get to the point where your business is performing at such a level that you do not need to be doing the day-to-day tasks to create revenue.

If you jump into different ideas and begin to take on more obligations, you will run yourself thin and will actually cause your primary income source to deteriorate. You will be thinking of so many ideas and add-on services that your mind will not be clear enough to focus on your main business.

I've seen this many times with other business owners I know. They want to have fifty businesses and have thousands of ideas of things they can and should do. Though this is a major trait of all entrepreneurs, it is also a vulnerability, a weakness that pulls you from concentrating where you should be and actually slows you down from achieving your initial goals.

Start with a core idea first. The main idea should be consuming all your focus and attention in the beginning stages of your business. Examine it, break it apart, and run through all scenarios to get proper growth. Gain the attention of your customers, build your brand, and create revenue coming in first. Once you have this key factor in place, you can then begin to build onto your brand to achieve horizontal success. The business' customer base and marketing reach will in turn help when launching other products, services, and businesses to complement the initial company or service.

If you don't focus your growth based on this process, you may inevitably fail. Picture it as an upside-down pyramid with a wide base on top that rests on your shoulders. With so many different factors happening all at once, it will eventually tip and come crumbling down. Instead, build vertically first, then expand your pyramid horizontally to support your main idea and revenue. A strong base is necessary before moving horizontally.

Keep in mind though that when you do start to expand into other areas, you need to eliminate focusing on corollaries that don't align with your specific skills. Though it may be an amazing idea and opportunity, it may just not be the right time to implement it. Hold on to and keep track of these thoughts and ideas as long-term plays that you will eventually get to down the road. Start with what you know and add in little by little as you grow.

If you are a home builder, you wouldn't want to jump into developing an entire neighborhood after your first build, would you? You need to use some common sense to add in horizontal growth to build upon until you are ready for larger leaps in business. Maybe you can start to incorporate custom designs, materials sourcing, or even other building-related services that you can offer within your company to tie in with your current processes. These little add-ons may eventually grow into large divisions of your company that will in turn build your entire organization to great heights.

There is a time and place for the next large step, and you will find it comes quicker than you think. Be patient with your growth by focusing on what you are good at and what can easily be added to your company profile to create extra revenue. You will get to a point when larger ideas and new businesses will be much easier to attain, and at this point, you will be able to achieve much quicker horizontal growth.

There was a time when building my business that I always wanted to get into investment and rental properties. When I was younger, I knew it would happen someday, but I didn't have the capital for down payments or renovation expenses. I was patient and began to offer additional services within my company that would eventually turn into separate divisions that were bringing in more revenue than I would have ever thought. I kept my nose to the ground and built as many complimentary services as I could.

Eventually I was fortunate enough to purchase my first property and cover all labor costs and renovation materials to transform this purchase into a money-making rental property. Fast forward several years later, that one idea of an additional opportunity had led to the acquisition of nine more properties, properties that allow me to employ staff year-round and create forced appreciation in real estate.

I had this idea early on but knew that the time was not right. I waited until the moment in time when capital was available and I had the staff to utilize this corollary opportunity. If I jumped in too early, it would have caused a major financial burden that I might have not been able to survive.

There is a time and a place for every corollary idea you have. Some can be implemented sooner than later, but never forget your goals to have as many opportunities as you would like. Keep track of these, be smart, and learn as much as you can before making that leap. The more training and knowledge you attain, the better success rates you inevitably will have when starting these corollary ideas to achieve horizontal growth.

I know you can achieve any level of success you work toward. You are your biggest cheerleader and biggest critic.

Plenty of people want to see you succeed and achieve financial freedom. I recommend sitting down with a good friend, a mentor, or maybe someone you admire and discussing your ideas and visions during this growth and new chapter of your life. You would be amazed when you have positive people in your life how much they want to help. They will shed new light and recommendations on your ideas and ways to avoid mistakes that they may have made in the past.

No matter what new venture or idea that I dream up, I always reach out to my core mentors to get their thoughts. Even if it is a quick five-minute phone call, their guidance and recommendations are always appreciated and valuable. When someone with a different viewpoint can listen to your ideas and provide feedback, you gain the advantage of multiple minds drumming up different ideologies, different challenges, and different ways to execute on those new concepts.

Before any new ventures, let's make sure that we focus first to establish your current business base of the pyramid. Ensure that you have a proper foundation with your company, your staff, and your clients. Once your essential level of support is properly built, it is time to start implementing corollary options to your organization.

Your circle of fellow entrepreneurs and mentors are here to help you. I am here to help you. We all want you to be successful and attain greatness. Once you have positive people that encourage and push you to become better, you cannot be stopped. You will grow in leaps and bounds personally and in your business venture. We are all rooting for you, so don't give up, dream big, and build your successful empire one corollary at a time.

Exercises:

1. List positive people who can help you in your pursuits.
2. Why do you want success?
3. What is driving you to build a business?
4. What aspects need to be put in place to finish your solid foundation?
5. Write down your big ideas. What it would take to achieve them?

CHAPTER 10

EXPERIENCED ENTREPRENEURS AND STAGNATION

———

"You are dying if you stay the same and don't change, you always have to be able to pivot"

- GUINIO VOLPONE

Guinio Volpone couldn't have stated this dilemma any better when we were together recently discussing business over a cocktail. Throughout the growth and creation of his large tech companies, Guinio was always pivoting in challenging or stagnant times. He realized that without change, there was no way to grow or expand business.

When business throws you a curve ball, you always have to be aware of your surroundings, be able to pivot, and be capable of changing directions to where the opportunities are. Whether it be to acquire or merge with another company or to simply find key areas of your industry that you can penetrate and conquer, there are plenty of ways to break out of stagnant growth.

For those readers who have been owning or operating in your space for quite some time, you may have different values and beliefs than those who can relate to the previous chapter. You've understood the struggles of getting past the beginning stages of business. You've scaled the initial hurdles that have kept many individuals from launching their products or services into the marketplace.

You've beaten the odds, but now what? Whether you have reached a plateau or are in a stagnant stage, the opportunity to achieve horizontal growth awaits, no matter the level of your current business. Continue to follow your core values in order to achieve this growth and success.

You have built your business upon your core values, hard work, and keeping your nose to the grindstone. However, to achieve horizontal success, you must focus on what truly makes you an entrepreneur: your drive, your ideas, and your desire to create.

Many of you are at a point in your business where you would like to improve and do better. You want to continue to create more and grow as an individual. If you are like me, you are on a constant quest for knowledge. Once you have mastered a skill, you are eager to continue learning and growing into the next one. We are always seeking a new goal to chase or a new opportunity to be created.

REASONS EXPERIENCED ENTREPRENEURS NEED TO EXPAND CHALLENGES

Just recently, I launched another company with my good friend and my company's mechanic. We found a void and an issue that could be improved with proper technology and equipment. We began to fabricate and construct mobile compressor units for the irrigation and construction industry, which previously had not had any improvements or innovation for quite some time. Our new products not only saved contractors time in their industry, they were also more mobile products at about half the price as the competition.

Without the yearning for knowledge and creation, we would not have dove into this new venture. We both were excited to learn new thought processes and to figure out problems from the ground up. From best practices and how to construct the perfect piece of equipment, we worked through development planning and issues to create a perfect piece of machinery.

I love this stuff! I love figuring out that something new is better than anything else on the market. While constructing, we constantly bounced ideas off of each other to figure the best way to make a streamlined product with the best constructed image made of the most efficient source of materials. It's a great feeling to start a new project and go through the thought process of dissecting and implementing revolutionary ideas. Once completed, we both felt an amazing sense of accomplishment that we had revolutionized something that no one else had thought of.

If you are reading this book, I know you have the same characteristics. You have the determination and drive to create and implement your ideas. Even if you have been in business for forty years, something deep down inside of you loves to tackle a challenge and start a new venture.

BREAKING STAGNATION

The entrepreneurial personality does not like to stay stagnant. It needs to feel challenged and express and implement new ideas through horizontal development into different avenues.

Don't let stagnation control your life. I know it is easy to do so once you have reached a certain level of comfort and happiness. I was once there too. I thought I was making great money with a successful company and began to get comfortable. This was a huge mistake and cost me at least a year or two from growing closer to my financial goals.

The risks of coasting and being stagnant are much costlier than they may appear. Not only are you creating a plateau mindset for your company and employees, but you are also forgetting the opportunity cost of not going after those new ideas, corollary options, or business dreams.

By taking the horizontal growth strategy sooner rather than later, you will see that your continual desire to pivot and expand comes easily. Once you are being supported by numerous revenue streams, you are more likely to be able to enjoy a more relaxed and successful lifestyle. These principal strategies will, in turn, help you achieve your goals.

The moment you begin to feel comfortable, you inhibit your ability to grow and cultivate new ideas. It is a virus that creeps into all entrepreneurs. You must never become stagnant or comfortable otherwise you will never get different results than those you are currently experiencing. It's time to step out of your comfort zone and start to stretch your brain. Stretch it and grow it so much that you are able to begin a new voyage of learning and struggles.

Without thinking of ideas about how to incorporate corollary options to your business or grow horizontally in different ventures, you will be stuck in your current life situation. You must focus on your values, your goals, and your deepest beliefs in life. These will all fuel your drive to break out of your current stagnation and propel you, your employees, and your businesses to success.

There is one key to successfully beating stagnation when looking for corollary opportunities. That key is to work harder—That's it! You've reached a stagnant stage because your work ethic has started to decline. It has started to allow you to feel comfortable and let your business run without your influence. Though this thought process is what many people think success is all about, it is not the true success of a horizontal entrepreneur.

I never want to feel comfortable, ever. I want to always have new challenges to work through and move on to the next level. I want to work on new projects and new ideas and to stretch my mind beyond its current capacity.

Even if I have a day when there isn't much on my calendar, I find things to do. I walk around the office and our warehouse and just start working. I will organize, clean, and think of ways to improve our current processes. By simply doing, your brain will start to come up with new ideas and concepts upon which you can capitalize. If you are sitting on your butt waiting for time to pass by, your brain will never look for new areas of growth. Keep yourself busy at all times throughout the day and night and continue to work no matter what the work is.

You've heard a body in motion stays in motion. Well, this pertains to your brain as well. The more you move and think, the more your brain will continue to formulate new ideas and positive implementations.

When you look at ways to incorporate simplification into your organization, you start to brainstorm and create new corollary options. You see this throughout the history of entrepreneurs that have become successful by creating an easier process to accomplish a simple task. They didn't invent the wheel; they just made a process more simplified and easier. They created ways for others to save time and money and in doing so created massive success.

Steve Jobs was quoted saying, "Simple can be harder than complex: You have to work hard to get your thinking clean to make it simple. But it's worth it in the end because once you get there, you can move mountains."[46]

Jobs is the epitome of simplifying to create wealth. He was able to take your camera, MP3 player, calendar, phone,

---

46 Neil Petch, "Simplification: The Entrepreneur's Secret to Success," *Entrepreneur*, February 7, 2016.

flashlight, and many more items and condense them all into something that fits in your pocket. By doing so, he gained massive success with over one billion active iPhone users around the world.[47]

Wrap your mind around that. If you were to simply make tasks easier for the consumer, you too could have your products in almost every household around the world.

All this starts by going through your day-to-day procedures and finding inefficiencies. Once the inefficiency is found, you can then formulate ideas and plans to reduce capital, reduce labor costs, and increase revenues.

PROBLEMS OF EXPERIENCED ENTREPRENEURS

An issue I see a lot of stagnant business owners struggle with is the desire to learn and create new corollary options. However, they don't know where to start. This is a common problem, but it is easily fixed if you know where to look. This goes back to the chapter on Looking for Corollaries. You must always think about your customers whenever feeling stuck in this quest to create.

If you go back, break down, and observe what your clientele's habits are, it won't be hard to brainstorm ideas on your next venture for horizontal growth. Get your management team together immediately and don't leave the conference room until you have come up with other ideas that will truly benefit your clients. If you don't have a management team,

---

47   Neil Cybart, "A Billion iPhone Users," *Above Avalon*, October 26, 2020.

then block off several hours in your calendar to go through all the traits that make you great and brainstorm what else you can offer to your customers. If you aren't able to think of new ideas, then you probably are not trying hard enough in your current line of work or need to change your direction of business altogether.

This is my favorite part of owning and running businesses. If I didn't have ways to dream up creating new business opportunities or sales avenues, I would be a miserable and boring person. Everywhere I go, I analyze and think of better processes and strategies for other people's businesses. I can't help it. It's something I constantly have going in the back of my mind, and I am always thinking of ways to improve.

I believe you are the same way. You know you can do better in the world and seek out ways to do so. You have the responsibility not only to yourself, but to your family and your employees to break out and continue to create new growth to build a larger enterprise.

You must always remember that people are counting on you, and staying in your comfort zone may inevitably let these people down. Like I mentioned before, I want my employees and people I love to be taken care of and live great lives. If you don't break free from being comfortable, you are letting all these people near and dear to you down. Many peers and people that you don't know yet will also be counting on you as you continue your journey to achieve horizontal success.

Never allow the thought "you have done all that you can do" into your mind. There are hundreds of excuses you could make. "I'm too old to start," "I'm too young," "I am busy with my kids," "I don't have enough time," and so on. Get those thoughts out of your head right now and change your mindset to figure out what you can do, not that you have done all you can. You need to continue to push yourself throughout your life.

Plenty of articles and books will help you to create a thriving positive mindset to bring you out of stagnation. In an article in *Entrepreneur* magazine's "How to Create a Growth Mindset," Jared Goetz, co-founder of 12th Bean, states that the first step out of stagnation, or a fixed mindset, is to admit to yourself that you are currently stuck. You can change or grow your mindset until this stage has been reached.[48]

Goetz goes on to identify steps to climb out of this fixed mindset. From acknowledging your weaknesses, seeking out opportunities, to continuing to learn and grow, you can beat stagnation and pivot into a promising direction.[49]

When I hear that entrepreneurs are plateauing, I believe they are simply content and satisfied with their current financial status. Anyone that tells me this makes me wonder why they are giving up so easily? There is always an opportunity to grow and change. Something can always be done to move forward in growth and development to enhance your business or businesses.

---

48 Jared Goetz, "How to Create a Growth Mindset as an Entrepreneur," *Entrepreneur,* December 11, 2018.

49 Ibid.

Did Colonel Sanders give up? Did John Paul DeJoria remain stagnant in his goals to build his business? Heck no! They continued to learn and push through all the roadblocks and obstacles life had to throw at them. They knew they were destined for greatness and being comfortable or giving up was never an option. They continued to persevere and build on their original ideas. They continued to find corollary opportunities to enhance their brands and their legacy.

Even writing this book right now is a corollary addition to my horizontal future plans. I was fortunate enough to go through the steps needed to build multiple businesses and offer hundreds of different products and services. Without pushing myself to build these organizations, I would not have had the courage to share my ideas and stories with you today.

Now I am starting a new journey to help as many entrepreneurs as I can maximize their lives and coach them to achieve diversified success. This book is just one way to help. I also offer coaching and mentoring services to other entrepreneurs to help them accomplish their goals in life. Many have said that I have been able to excel them ten-fold in their business growth by sharing what works, what doesn't work, and where to focus their attention.

If I had not had the idea to help others through another avenue of my ventures, I would be doing the world a disservice. I feel obligated to help as many people as possible before I leave this earth. This is a corollary goal of mine. By using my knowledge, skills, and ability to analyze, I have created a new opportunity in which I help others to follow in my footsteps and accomplish their own horizontal growth. This book is a way I found that can easily reach the largest amount of like-minded individuals across the world, and I will continue to share with you all how to take your businesses and lives to the next level.

The time is now. It's time to step up and break the stagnate chains on your life and your business. It's time to go to work and build upon the business you once started and now take over the marketplace. It's time to prove to yourself and to everyone else that you won't become a statistic, that you will provide for your employees, your family, and your community. Let's get back to the drive you once had and the passion to grow your knowledge and your abilities. Kick stagnation to the curb, and let's get back to the grindstone to create new ideas, new corollaries, and new businesses to build the biggest damn empire you are destined to have!

Exercises:

1. What is keeping you from the next step?
2. List out everything that is holding you back from reaching your goals.
3. What are you willing to implement to improve your mental growth?
4. Write down a list of duties you can perform when you are feeling stuck to keep your mind and body active.

CONCLUSION

———

So what now? With the current state of the economy, we are not close to a normal market by a long shot. In the recent COVID-19 pandemic, companies are struggling to stay afloat, businesses are shutting down, yet others seem to be prospering. But how is that possible you may be asking?

Without bringing up the politics of local governments that may be restricting certain states over others, I believe that the entrepreneurs that are able to flourish during our current state of the world are doing so through horizontal growth. Whenever tough times occur, we as entrepreneurs find a way to pivot and focus on solutions. Solutions that lead to opportunities for further diversifying our brands and our organizations.

The problem with the current turmoil of the world is that most people are focused on their one product or service. These business owners continue to think vertically and in the short term. In doing so, they don't realize they are working harder and not smarter. Their days are working them; they aren't working their days. They are capping their destined ability to be great. We need to break these weights that hold people down to start viewing the world and marketplace in a horizontal manner.

I truly do not want any of you to become one of the 33 percent of businesses that fail within ten years. I honestly want to help you get through tough times, expand your knowledge, and achieve the level of success for which you were destined. By implementing the horizontal mentality in this book, I believe you can have anything you want in life and be able to weather any sort of economic turmoil.

In the end, what good is it to have the knowledge to be successful if you cannot bring any other successful people with you on your journey? I want to bring you on that journey. It's time to make the choice and start moving in the right direction.

The evidence is there. If people like Warren Buffett and John Paul DeJoria are able to manage multiple successful companies and offer a wide array of products and services, you can too. Utilize your strengths, your assets, and your staff to propel you to new endeavors.

The time is now. Whether there is a natural disaster, a worldwide pandemic, or an economic recession, there is no better time to begin implementing these ideas and strategies. Make a commitment to yourself, your family, your friends, and your employees that you want to succeed and make a change. Pivot and push yourself to begin your diversification quest.

Whether you are sixteen or seventy years old, there is still time to commit and start planning out your corollary opportunities. Find your personal flow state and become obsessed to seek out opportunities to implement. Add in additional products and services and when the time is right explore the larger add-on opportunities to start new businesses and ventures.

By listening to your clients and offering them what they seek, you will be able to increase your business exponentially. These corollaries will grow and create new revenue streams, new levels of business, and above all, new successes. You will be able to upsell, cross-sell, and emerge into new industries throughout your market.

Although this entire process may seem daunting and like a hassle, no matter what, you must keep it simple. Seek out ways to simplify your business and industry. At this point, you will realize where to focus your attention and resources.

Through this quest, you will be able to create numerous jobs for talented individuals that will in return help you to build your empire. You will soon find out that bringing great team members with you along this voyage is one of the most satisfying feelings you will ever have as a business owner.

The impression you will create and lives you will change will forever be on your personal resume. You will be remembered for what you were able to accomplish and all the lives you impacted and continue to impact through a bigger thinking mentality. When I leave this earth, I want my tombstone to read, "James Manske, a man that impacted and helped many lives."

What do you want to be left with your name and your legacy?

For me personally, this is one of my biggest key points for my pride and motivation. I am truly blessed to have the team, family, friends, and mentors I have and to be able to connect with so many talented people throughout my life. I am grateful to be sharing my knowledge on the process of horizontal growth with you in hopes that you too can have the pleasure to experience these feelings as well.

Throughout the process of writing this book, I have grown as an entrepreneur by realizing all the great things I have already accomplished in my life thus far. At times, I forget to look back and realize where I have come from and what I had to get through to be where I am today. After sharing my stories and teachings with you, I have a sense of revitalization to push harder and continue my personal growth.

I want you to feel the same sense of accomplishment and reach the success you were destined for. Rise above the competition and be that person of influence you have always dreamed of being. The time is now to break from the ordinary to become extraordinary. Let's go and create a beautiful future of success together.

Cheers!

ACKNOWLEDGEMENTS

———

I would like to acknowledge all the great individuals who have helped me with this amazing journey.

To the amazing mentors and friends that have been in my life and provided stories in this book including:

Ron Carson, Travis Freeman, Kim and Jill Wolfe, Van Deeb, Guinio Volpone, and Achim Romanowski

Your mentorship and willingness to help and pull others to success with forever be appreciated by myself and many others.

Special thanks to Eric Koester and everyone at The Creator Institute including Brian Bies, my personal editors Whitney Jones, Carol McKibben and team, New Degree Press, and everyone else that helped make this book possible.

I would also like to acknowledge my amazing family and friends that made this book possible with their support and encouragements:

Aaron Arsenault
Achim Romanowski
Alicia Champion
Amy Dritley
Anahita Nikseresht
Andrea Zahourek
Andrew Goranson
Andrew Sigerson
Ashley Livengood
Ben Mathes
Benjamin Steward
Brenda Sedivy
Brian Huddleston
Carole Sprunk
Chad Hayden
Charles Sederstrom
Chris Jones
Chris Manske
Chris Richardson
Christopher and Clara
Senkbile
CJ Monahan
Collin Monzon
Connor Russell
Corina Nelson
Craig Keiser
Cyrus Jaffery
Dan Waters
Daniel Sundermeier
Danny Stone
David Comeau
Devin Beach

Doug and Muriel Manske
Dudley & Jacob Reis
Dustin Messersmith
Eric Flores
Eric Koester
Evan Lamprecht
Genice Chochon
Glen Thieman
Greg Hanson
Jacob Bieber
Jacob Zadalis
Jamey Conrad
Jay Oxton
Jay Manske
Jack and Kathy Manske
Jeff Grewe
Jonathan Patton
Joseph Scoville
Josh Brink
Josh Barker
Julie Lentz
Justin Thiesse
Kari Ketcham
Kathy Rygg
Katie Eikmeier
Kevin Bender
Kyle Bacus
Kyle Brau
Luke Reifenrath
Madison Carson
Mandy Lassek
Marla Snyder

McCallister Maurer
Melvin Stuart
Michael & Stephanie
Borman
Mike Raines
Nancy Sohns
Nick Wimmer
Nicole Bianchi
Nikki Thomsen
Patrick Niebauer
Paul J Bieber
Paul Sanchez
Rachel Irwin
Rick and Kelli Duvall
Rita Rasmussen

Rob DuVall
Ryan Pettit
Sara Kohll
Sarah Ohrt
Shawn Falcone
Sue Henson
Sue Beckman
Susan E Gottsch
Tara Gipper
Todd Schneidewind
Travis Freeman
Van Deeb
Will Morales
William Manske
Zach Winkel

APPENDIX

INTRODUCTION

Deane, Michael T. "Top 6 Reasons New Businesses Fail," *Investopedia*, February 28, 2020. https://www.investopedia.com/financial-edge/1010/top-6-reasons-new-businesses-fail.aspx-#citation-1.

FrogDog Magazine. "Strategies for Growth." January 6, 2016. https://www.frog-dog.com/magazine/strategies-for-growth#.

CHAPTER 1

Collins, Bryan. "3 Surprising Benefits of Flow State," *Forbes*, March 31, 2020. https://www.forbes.com/sites/bryancollinseurope/2020/03/31/3-surprising-benefits-of-flow-state/?sh=-31f900af3627.

Koerner, Alexander. "John Paul Dejoria's Journey from Homeless to Billionaire." *NBC News,* May 30, 2018. https://www.nbcnews.com/know-your-value/feature/john-paul-dejoria-s-journey-homeless-billionaire-ncna825246.

Omar Elattar & The Passionate Few. "How I Became a Billionaire after Being Broke & Homeless Twice (John Paul DeJoria Interview)." January 28, 2019. Video, 53:53. https://www.youtube.com/watch?v=-ggEBOTAKr8&t=2116s.

Quotes Memo. "Sumner Redstone Quotes." Accessed December 20, 2020. https://www.quotesmemo.com/author-sumner-redstone/.

CHAPTER 2

Kaufman, Karl. "Here's Why Warren Buffett and Other Great Investors Don't Diversify." *Forbes,* July 24, 2018. https://www.forbes.com/sites/karlkaufman/2018/07/24/heres-why-warren-buffett-and-other-great-investors-dont-diversify/?sh=77e9d27b4795.

Lexico Online. s.v. "Diverse (Adj.)." Accessed December 21, 2020, https://www.lexico.com/en/definition/diverse.

"The 2017 DNA of an Entrepreneur Report." *Hiscox* (blog), September 12, 2017. https://www.hiscox.com/blog/2017-dna-of-an-entrepreneur-report.

CHAPTER 3

Heasman, Chris. "The Tragic, Real-Life Story of Colonel Sanders." *Mashed,* August 12, 2018. https://www.mashed.com/131055/the-tragic-real-life-story-of-colonel-sanders/.

Mayberry, Matt. "Don't Lose That All-Important Sense of Urgency. Do It—Now!" *Entrepreneur Magazine,* May 14, 2016. https://www.entrepreneur.com/article/275783.

Nafte, Dennis. "Colonel Sanders Failed 1009 Times before Succeeding." *Medium*, September 10, 2017. https://medium.com/@dennisnafte/colonel-sanders-failed-1009-times-before-succeeding-ac5492a5c191.

Swant, Marty. "The World's Most Valuable Brands." *Forbes*, Accessed January 16, 2021. https://www.forbes.com/the-worlds-most-valuable-brands/#a1f4351119c0.

CHAPTER 4

Nagarajan, Shalini. "'The Market Doesn't Care Who You Are': 11 of JPMorgan CEO Jamie Dimon's Best Quotes." *Business Insider*, June 17, 2020. https://markets.businessinsider.com/news/stocks/jamie-dimon-best-quotes-businesses-tend-pass-costs-customers-2020-6-1029318462.

Omar Elattar & The Passionate Few. "How I Became a Billionaire after Being Broke & Homeless Twice (John Paul DeJoria Interview)." January 28, 2019. Video, 53:53. https://www.youtube.com/watch?v=-ggEBOTAKr8&t=2116s. *Starbucks Corporation.* "Starbucks Fiscal 2019 Annual Report." Accessed December 14, 2020. https://s22.q4cdn.com/869488222/files/doc_financials/2019/2019-Annual-Report.pdf.

World Population Review. "GDP Ranked by Country 2020." Accessed January 17, 2021. https://worldpopulationreview.com/countries/countries-by-gdp.

CHAPTER 5

Hull, Patrick. "Don't Get Lazy about Your Client Relationships." *Forbes,* December 6, 2013. https://www.forbes.com/sites/patrickhull/2013/12/06/tools-for-entrepreneurs-to-retain-clients/?sh=62c086b42443.

Manoukian, Julia. "The Psychology of Luxury Car Buyers: 7 Considerations." *Limelight,* November 27, 2019. https://www.limelightplatform.com/blog/psychology-luxury-car-buyers-considerations.

Reichheld, Fred. "Prescription for Cutting Costs." *Bain & Company.* Accessed October 25, 2020. https://media.bain.com/Images/BB_Prescription_cutting_costs.pdf.

Williams, Brian. "21 Mind-Blowing Sales Stats." *The Brevet Group.* Accessed October 26, 2020. https://blog.thebrevetgroup.com/21-mind-blowing-sales-stats.

CHAPTER 6

All Great Quotes. "Tom Peters Quotes." Accessed October 15, 2020. https://www.allgreatquotes.com/quote-440881/.

Breeden, Alice, and Adam Howe. "Why Simplicity Is the Key to Accelerating Performance." *Heidrick & Struggles,* December 5, 2019. https://www.heidrick.com/Knowledge-Center/Publication/Why_simplicity_is_the_key_to_accelerating_performance.

Daffern, Josh. "Seven Great Quotes from the Chick-Fil-a Leadercast." *Patheos,* May 13, 2013. https://www.patheos.com/blogs/

newwineskins/seven-great-quotes-from-the-chick-fil-a-lead-ercast/.

Shashi, Sarvesh. "How Not to Complicate—Keeping Entrepreneurship Simple." *Entrepreneurship India,* September 3, 2018. https://www.entrepreneur.com/article/319415.

CHAPTER 7

Keller, Scott, and Meaney, Mary. "Attracting and Retaining the Right Talent," *McKinsey & Company,* November 24, 2017. https://www.mckinsey.com/business-functions/organization/our-insights/attracting-and-retaining-the-right-talent#.

Keller, Wendy. "The 3-Step Process to Hiring Your First Assistant." *The Hour,* November 29, 2018. https://www.thehour.com/news/article/The-3-Step-Process-to-Hiring-Your-First-Assistant-13428773.php.

CHAPTER 8

Chen, Andrew. "Know the Difference between Data-Informed and versus Data-Driven." *@andrewchen Newsletter,* Accessed October 7, 2020. https://andrewchen.co/know-the-difference-between-data-informed-and-versus-data-driven/.

Iqbal, Mansoor. "Uber Revenue and Usage Statistics (2020)." *Business of Apps,* October 30, 2020. https://www.businessofapps.com/data/uber-statistics/.

Lloyd, Viola. "Turning Data into Insight." *HRD The HR Director,* August 8, 2016. https://www.thehrdirector.com/features/hr-in-business/turning-data-into-insight/#.

Zhange, Shu, and Shih, Gerry, "Uber Seen Reaching $10.8 Billion in Bookings in 2015: Fundraising Presentation." *Reuters,* August 21, 2015. https://www.reuters.com/article/us-uber-tech-fundraising/uber-seen-reaching-10-8-billion-in-bookings-in-2015-fundraising-presentation-idUSKCN0QQ0G320150821.

CHAPTER 9

Bolt, Chandler. "4 Pearls of Wisdom from Inspirational Entrepreneurs." *Influencive,* November 20th, 2019. https://www.influencive.com/4-pearls-of-wisdom-from-inspirational-entrepreneurs/#.

Kabov, Anatole. "What the Best in the Business Have to Say about Succeeding." *LinkedIn,* August 14, 2017. https://www.linkedin.com/pulse/what-best-business-have-say-succeeding-anatole-kabov/.

Robinson, Ryan. "60 Entrepreneurs Share Their Best Business Advice." *Just Luminate,* Accessed October 29, 2020. https://justluminate.com/article/1586668/60-entrepreneurs-share-their-best-business-advice.

Taylor, Leslie. "Are Entrepreneurs Born or Made?" *Inc,* October 24, 2006. https://www.inc.com/news/articles/200610/born.html.

Wei, Jessica. *Due,* January 3, 2016. https://due.com/blog/the-best-revenge-is-massive-success-frank-sinatra/.

CHAPTER 10

Cybart, Neil. "A Billion iPhone Users." *Above Avalon,* October 26, 2020. https://www.aboveavalon.com/notes/2020/10/26/a-billion-iphone-users.

Goetz, Jared. "How to Create a Growth Mindset as an Entrepreneur." *Entrepreneur,* December 11, 2018. https://www.entrepreneur.com/article/324071.

Petch, Neil. "Simplification: The Entrepreneur's Secret to Success." *Entrepreneur,* February 7, 2016. https://www.entrepreneur.com/article/270387.